"Dr. Jeffery Hampton is 'The (personally attest to this; during the eleven y.... ve battled cancer, through his ministry, Dr. Hampton has inspired and comforted me. His concern and caring is a great gift that can be experienced through his sermons."

– Mauleene Broadwater, Lay Member,
Pulaski Heights United Methodist Church

"By his caring attitude and his active care of members of our congregation, we have been so blessed to have the ministry of this good man, Dr. Jeff Hampton. His message from the pulpit has blessed us, but—so much more—his daily care has been an example to all."

– Martha Ann Fox, Lay Member,
Pulaski Heights United Methodist Church

"Rev. Hampton's fine meditations speak to a variety of needs within the faith community."

– Rex Ellis, Ordained Baptist Minister,
Virginia

Meditations
in
Black
&
White

Beyond
the
Comfort
Zone

Jeffery B. Hampton, D.Min.

Parkhurst Brothers, Inc., Publishers

LITTLE ROCK

www.parkhurstbrothers.com
Copies of this and other Parkhurst Brothers Inc., Publishers titles are available to organizations and corporations for purchase in quantity by contacting Special Sales Department at our home office location, listed on our web site.

Printed in the United States of America
Original Trade Paperback * First Edition, 2012

2012 2013 2014 2015 2016   12 11 10 9 8 7 6 5
4 3 2 1
For Library of Congress Cataloging-in-Publication Data, please consult the publisher's website after the month of publication.

ISBN: Trade Paperback   978-1-935166-60-3   [10 digit: 1-935166-60-3]
ISBN: e-book 978-1-935166-59-7   [10-digit: 1-935166-59-X]

This book is printed on archival-quality paper that meets requirements of the American National Standard for Information Sciences, Permanence of Paper, Printed Library Materials, ANSI Z39.48-1984.

Acquired for Parkhurst Brothers Publishers by: Ted Parkhurst
Editor: Barbara Paddack
Cover design and page design: Harvill-Ross Studios
Back cover photo: Arthur Paul Bowen
Author's Note: All of my meditations use the The Holy Bible, containing The Old & New Testaments, New Revised Standard Version, Anglicized Edition-Copyright 1989, 1995-National Council of Churches of Christ in the USA, Cambridge-University Press, First Published 2008, (www.cambridge.org).

In Loving Memory of my mother,
who encouraged me
to step beyond my comfort zone:

Dr. Nora Lee Banks Hampton
(1935-1999)

This book is dedicated to my wife,
the love of my life,
and our two daughters:

Cynthia
Joya and Cheyanne

I am very thankful for the loving support of my family: My parents, Dr. R.J. and Regina Stewart Hampton; my brother, sister, and niece, Tim Hampton, Regina Hampton, and Kelsey Hampton Newman; my in -laws and brother- in -law, John and Dorothy Puckett, and Stephen Puckett. I am indebted to Elizabeth Holley for editing and for her overall help with this project.

And finally, to the wonderful membership and friends of Pulaski Heights United Methodist Church in Little Rock, Arkansas, who have given me the opportunity to serve as one of their associate pastors. They have taught me what it truly means to reach out locally and around the world, and how to care elaborately for one another!

CONTENTS

Preface

As an African-American pastor who has experienced the challenge of finding new footing in a setting beyond my comfort zone, I have experienced how God can stretch the heart. The meditations in this book are the result of that heart-stretching—a series of studies that are both orthodox and consistent with Christian teaching. While I have felt God stretching my heart and expanding my vision of what it means to be a Christian, I have also felt the great Comforter, the Holy Spirit. The Spirit has led me to challenge you, my reader, to examine your own comfort zone, not in the light of Jeff Hampton's experience, but in the light of God's Word and the Holy Spirit's individual message to you. May you find new life in His Word, a life that expands each time you listen to the Holy Spirit and take that next, tentative step in your life of grace.

In this book, I will attempt to demystify Jesus Christ's Good News of hope and inclusivity. In the fall of 1976 I received my call to ordained ministry. On November 19, 1976, at the age of 15, I preached my first sermon at St. John A.M.E. Church in Fordyce, Arkansas. By the fall of 1977 I was assigned as pastor of Greater St. Mark A.M.E. Church in Thornton, Arkansas. In the fall of 1984, I was assigned to St. Paul A.M.E. Church in Newport, Arkansas. In June of 1990 I was appointed to the Ebenezer UMC Conway- Mount Zion Center Ridge- Wesley UMC Morrilton Charge. Three years later, I was appointed to McCabe Chapel UMC in North Little Rock, Arkansas. In June of 1999 I was appointed one of the associate pastors of Pulaski Heights UMC in Little Rock, Arkansas. I was not able to see either Greater St. Mark or Pulaski Heights until the day I arrived.

After almost 36 years of ministry, I am pleased with the measure of my faith response. At the present time I find myself serving at a level of which I never dreamed. I have learned to keep an open heart and open mind to the Spirit of God.

My African-American faith tradition has always fought for the rights of minorities, and all people, but the circle of those needing to experience justice and political freedom continues to grow around the world. I am inclusive and faithful to the example of Jesus' ministry to all persons by reaching out to people regardless of age, disabilities, race, color, national origin, sexual orientation, economic condition or status. "Inclusiveness means openness, acceptance and support that enables all persons to participate in the life of the church, the community and the world. Thus, inclusiveness denies every semblance of discrimination" (The 2008 Book of Discipline of the United Methodist Church, section VI, 139).

I am so thankful for the wonderful membership and friends of Pulaski Heights United Methodist Church in Little Rock, Arkansas, for the opportunity to serve and share the "Good News" as one of their pastors.

Jeffery B. Hampton

Foreword

It has been more than 12 years ago that Jeff was appointed to Pulaski Heights United Methodist Church in Little Rock, Arkansas, where he is presently serving as the associate/executive pastor in charge of the broad areas of caring ministries and the program staff, for this 4,000-member congregation.

With the news of this appointment, I experienced very strong mixed emotions. I was very proud as a father would naturally be, but at the same time I was very apprehensive because the United Methodist cross-racial movement had not previously been always successful. The problems encountered are not racial but cultural, and cultural problems are insidious and evasive. The fearless move to temporarily break with your past tradition/community and the comfort it affords is insidiously debilitating, but Jeff has thrived.

As a father I often urged Jeff to share his experiences and discomfort that could be part of a road map as the United Methodist Church continues its bold movement in church growth.

Jeff does this in his book "Meditations in Black and White: Beyond the Comfort Zone." Nothing mirrors a preacher's joys, frustration, ambitions and faith more than his sermons, because a preacher always preaches first to himself.

Dr. Reginald J. Hampton

My Second Son

So young, so promising, so warm;
So sensitive, so strong;
Just another kid in the eyes of others,
But to me, this is my son.

So caring, so unselfish, so God Fearing;
So wise to be so young;
Perhaps an average young man to others,
But this is how I see my son.

So thoughtful, so truthful, so committed,
So very much a parson born;
One of millions of kids to the world,
But to me, he's my second son.

But I have never been worried
About any of my children,
And that period they call fool's hill;
Because I know the kind of father I've been,
And I know who their mother is!

–The Rev. Dr. Reginald J. Hampton (1985)

Introduction

When it was announced that Jeff – or should I say Dr. Jeffery Hampton – was being appointed to the very liberal, very large and very old Pulaski Heights United Methodist Church in Little Rock, Arkansas – only a few in the congregation were surprised or concerned. We were the perfect church for just such an appointment. In fact, we were and we are.

Oh yes, there were some surprises, as there are with any new appointment. When his first sermons were based more on intellectual theology rather than emotional traditions associated with African-American Methodism, we adjusted easily. In fact, we learned that if we listened well to every word from Dr. Jeff, our lives were changed and our love for others expanded.

And that is what will happen to you as you read and maybe even reread these thoughts and meditations from Dr. Jeff to his new, almost all-white congregation. Thoughts from a God-loving young man who went through troubling and difficult times growing up. Who was raised in a household and a community where the word, inclusiveness, became the byword for almost all professing Christians.

So don't read these words in a haphazard manner. As you read, think about what it was like for Dr. Jeff and his strange congregation to live together under the blanket of new world theology always thinking about their Lord and what He would have them be or become in this wonderful new world of ours.

–Bob Sells, Lay Member,
  Pulaski Heights United Methodist Church

CHAPTER ONE

Jeremiah Surveys the Potter's House

Jeremiah 18:1-6

Why did God invite Jeremiah to take a spiritual field trip to survey a potter's house? Jeremiah enjoyed a personal relationship with God, and he was always seeking a better understanding of his faith.

The Prophet Jeremiah was a dramatic person who would have been very hard to ignore during his time. We know about Jeremiah partly because of the many dictations he made to his assistant. Jeremiah could see doom in store for his people. Many of the people were spiritually weak. The godless and egotistical king, political leaders, and the other prophets and the priests were all against Jeremiah because of God's message.

Jeremiah is considered by some to be the pioneer prophet of personal religion. He endured many personal trials from the beginning of his ministry until the end of his life. His prophetic exhortations for Judah and Jerusalem concerning faithfulness and disobedience, good and evil, and rewards and punishment, guaranteed him many enemies. His foes considered him to be conceited and arrogant. The prophet Jeremiah can best be described as a sensitive, loving poet from a priestly family, who was deeply devoted to God from the days of his youth. Jeremiah said he experienced the voice of God telling him that he was known to God even while he was yet in his mother's womb, that he was consecrated to God's work—to be a prophet—before he was born (Jer. 1:4-5).

The prophet Jeremiah teaches and demonstrates the high and low moments of a personal relationship with God. God is presented as being very interested and involved in the lives of the people. Jeremiah was born four miles northeast of Jerusalem. He is often referred to as the "Weeping Prophet" because of his mourning and tears for the destruction of Jerusalem that was to come. The northern kingdom of Israel, with its capital at Samaria, had fallen. Judah and Jerusalem would soon fall for not obeying the words of the Lord. The "Weeping Prophet" said:

Is there no balm in Gilead? Is there no physician there? Why then has the health of my poor people not been restored? O that my head were a spring of water, and my eyes a fountain of tears, so that I might weep day and night for the slain of my poor people (Jer. 8:22; 9:1)!

Jeremiah had an ongoing personal spiritual struggle with God. Nevertheless, God's people must return to God, regardless of the journey, in order to have a fulfilling and enduring relationship with God. One day Jeremiah became so frustrated with his personal feelings and the messages that God was placing on his heart that he accused God of deceiving him. Imagine Jeremiah's lament, which went something like this:

Lord, you have made me a joke to the citizens. They mock me when I cry for the destruction that is to come. Your Word has become my undoing, as my peers deride me and make fun of me in public. In spite of the contempt heaped upon me, Lord, you know I cannot contain your Word, but must proclaim it to the people (Jer. 20:7-9).

This is a brief glimpse of the man Jeremiah, and his

personal relationship with God as he struggled to be obedient and faithful.

After many complaints and laments, the Lord says to the "Weeping Prophet," in Jeremiah 18: 2-3, and I paraphrase, let's go together to the house of the pot maker. I will speak there and you may consider what I have to say. We went together to the potter's house, where we found the potter at work at his wheel. Like all potters of the day, he was probably fashioning containers for food and perhaps for carrying water from the well to the home. Jeremiah did not witness anything new when he first surveyed the potter's house. He saw a potter, at the potter's wheel, molding clay into pots and vessels of different shapes and sizes. During Jeremiah's time in history a potter's wheel probably consisted of two horizontal circular stone disks bound together. The lower disk was attached to a simple mechanism that allowed the disk to be rotated from underneath by the potter's feet. The upper disk or wheel on the same axle supported a large round lump of prepared clay. The potter set the wheel in motion. Working from the top of the lump of clay, the potter sent one hand down into the clay mass to shape the inside of the vessel that was being formed, while the other hand skillfully fashioned the outside. The potter kept the wheel turning, first slowly, then faster, then slowly, using the strength of his feet to "bend" the clay and the skill of his hands to create the vessel. Close to the potter there was probably a container of water that the potter would dip his hands into to smooth the clay as it whirled on the wheel. A beautiful vessel was developing in the hands of the potter. Jeremiah surveyed the potter's patience, intimate involvement and delicate skills.

Suddenly, the potter stops and notices that the vessel has

an imperfection. It is spoiled or broken in the potter's hand. Jeremiah witnesses the potter's confidence as the vessel is smashed into a lump of clay again. The wheel starts to turn again, and another vessel is made that is pleasing to the potter.

Jeremiah reports, and again I paraphrase, then I remembered the scripture and its rhetorical question: can the Lord not do with Israel just as the potter has done with his misshapen pot and cast it away? Even as the clay is subject to the potter's satisfaction, isn't it within the Lord's power to accept or reject the people of Israel? Read the passage in Jeremiah 18:5-6 and meditate on the relationship of Israel to the Lord. Then consider your own relationship with God.

It was at this moment that Jeremiah realized what God was revealing and teaching him. It was the realization that Judah, although it was "a spoiled vessel," was still in the hands of God, a God of infinite resourcefulness and enduring love. The purpose of God was not defeated. The Divine Potter loves the clay. From this time forward, while not ceasing to proclaim the destructive judgment of God, Jeremiah began to preach, as well, that beyond certain judgment for Judah, God also promised them a future with hope.

The potter's house also demonstrated to Jeremiah the sovereignty of God. There is a Divine will, as well as a human free will. Sometimes our human nature frustrates the purpose of God. But God is not in a hurry, and God's will for the perfection of all nations is only matched by God's patience. When the prophet Jeremiah realized that Judah lay in God's hands like a spoiled vessel in the hands of the potter, he knew that after the destruction the nation was to be reconciled to God and made over into a new people. He knew that God would redeem the remnant of Israel and write the law upon their hearts.

The image of the potter and the clay appears to have originated with Jeremiah. The image of God as potter can also be found in Genesis 2:7 which says that the Lord made mankind out of the dirt we walk on, "the dust of the ground."

Adelaide Pollard, a Christian activist, penned this text during a time of personal despair. The message centers on completely forsaking self and submitting to God's will:

Have thine own way, Lord! Have thine own way!
Thou art the potter; I am the clay.
Mold me and make me after thy will,
While I am waiting, yielded and still.

Psalm 46:10a, "Be still, and know that I am God!"

Questions for Reflection and Meditation

• Can I trust that God has a plan for my life even if I am a broken "vessel"?

• In light of the experiences of Jeremiah, and his personal relationship with God as the potter, how do I see my personal relationship with God, my family relationships, my spiritual formation and my individual journey?

• Have I, like Jeremiah, ever experienced derision because others misinterpreted my motives in serving God?

• What does it mean to you that God made you out of the dust of the ground? Do you find comfort or disquiet in that image?

CHAPTER TWO

Equal Compensation for Christian Discipleship

Matthew 20:1-16

Prayer: God of all creation, your grace is truly amazing; bless us to see beyond our personal needs and to see the needs of others. Amen.

What can we learn from the parable is known as "The Laborers in the Vineyard?" Sometimes hard working Christians who have labored in the church during difficult times as well as during good times find this passage of scripture troubling. One can read into this passage several interpretations. Many theologians say that Matthew 20:1-16 refers to the different periods of a person's life in which one may respond to the Lord. Some say that the workers first called are the Jews, and those called last are the Gentiles. Others might say that this parable represents the whole gospel age up to Christ's return, and the workers are groups saved at various periods. Others say that the first are the Old Testament saints and those called at later times are the apostles. The explanations are varied and many.

The setting of this parable, as described by Matthew, is the key to its understanding. Jesus had just been approached by the "Rich Young Ruler" with a question concerning eternal life. Jesus invites the young man to forsake all and follow him, but the rich young ruler chooses to keep what he has and walks away sorrowful. After a brief discussion concerning the Kingdom of Heaven, Peter, who is well known for speaking out, steps forward to remind Jesus that he and some of the disciples had left and forsaken all to follow him. Peter seems to want to emphasize to Jesus that, unlike the rich young ruler who had just walked away, he is steadfast. So Peter asked Jesus a pivotal question: What will be the rewards for a stalwart service like Matthew? Read it yourself, in your own Bible, Matthew 19:27b). It is at this moment that Jesus looks at Peter and says, and I paraphrase, "When we meet in Heaven, you will find me seated next to The Holy One as judgment is pronounced on the people of Israel. Many will have suffered loss for me, but on that day they will be repaid a hundred times over." (Matthew 19:28).

Imagine Peter and the other disciples swelling with pride. Imagine their shared sense of having made all the right decisions. Jesus then tells Peter that those who have been first in this world will be last in the next and those who have been last in this world will be first in the next (Matthew 19:30).

This statement is so important that Matthew reports that Jesus uses the same statement to introduce "The Labors in the Vineyard" and to conclude the parable. Jesus then tells His disciples that the Kingdom of Heaven is like a landowner who went out early in the morning to hire laborers for his vineyard. The landowner contracted to pay the first workers a good daily wage. The landowner then returned to the marketplace four more times; at 9 a.m., noon, 3 p.m. and even as late as 5 p.m. Each later visit to the marketplace produced workers, but the landowner did not say how much he would pay them, only that it would be a fair wage. At 6 p.m., those who started working the latest were paid first. The landowner paid a full-day's wage to the workers who were hired at 5 p.m. that very day. The biblical term for their pay is called "grace," an undeserved gift.

Watching this process were the laborers that were hired early that morning. They had worked hard all day in the grueling heat, but they, too, received the same daily wage as those who were hired in the late evening. The first workers were irritated and they complained. The landowner responds by saying he paid them according to their agreement, and that it was his right to be gracious to the late comers if he chose to do so. "So the last will be first, and the first will be last" (Matthew 20:16).

Jesus tells this parable in response to Peter's question, "What then will we have?" And Jesus' basic response is that you and all that follow will have "equal compensation for Christian discipleship."

The first workers in this parable appear to represent the apostles and others who are called by Christ early in life and labor long and hard in the "vineyard." The other workers in the vineyard are those who hear and respond to the gospel later in life and do not have the opportunity to do as much service.

In this parable, everyone that accepts Christian discipleship receives more than what is fair. No one has the right to question the generosity of God. And those who serve long and hard should not be envious if others receive the same reward. Many Christians may have these feelings at one time or another.

The workers who arrived late at the vineyard were people who had not been hired. They accepted the invitation as soon as they heard it at the end of the day. Many are without a place of service in the vineyard today, because no one has invited them to work.

When called by the gospel to serve, we should say yes at once. And once given the opportunity, we should work diligently for the time we have left – living the rest of our lives in grateful service to God.

Jesus' parable of those who labored in the vineyard demonstrates for us that there is no room in the Kingdom of Heaven for those who are envious or for those who seek more than an eternal relationship with God. We must find peace with God's methods of measurement and not insist upon methods of reward that make sense to us, in our limited, worldly understanding.

Questions for Reflection and Meditation

• Am I content with the terms and rewards of my servanthood?

• Am I ever jealous of others in my congregation, of co-workers, or those outside of the workforce?

• How has God shown his free gift of grace in my life, in the lives of my parents or siblings or children?

• When was the last time I questioned God's generosity to others?

CHAPTER THREE

God Answers Habakkuk

Habakkuk 2:1-4

Habakkuk is honestly confronting the problem of why a just God appears to stand by silently when evil people seem to dominate others who are clearly more righteous. In Habakkuk 1:13b, this perpetual question is played out in a very dramatic way. The prophet receives an answer that is eternally valid: God is still sovereign, and in God's own way and at the proper time will deal with the wicked; and until we come to understand God's logic, we must find peace in living by faith. That message of believing until we comprehend is plainly laid out in Habakkuk 2:4b.

Prayer: God of the ages, God of a thousand generations, thank you for giving us this lifetime. In these quiet moments we gather our thoughts to give you thanksgiving and praise, as well as to intercede for others who are in need. Our prayers are for those who are unhappy and for those who are suffering. Lord stand among us blessing us and keeping us. Reveal the Good News of your Word to us, in his name we pray. Amen.

Very little is known about the prophet Habakkuk. His name means "embracer," which scholars suggest spoke symbolically of his "wrestling with God" or "embracing the philosophical problems of the nation." Professional prophets like Habakkuk exercised great influence upon Israel from the time of Samuel. They not only expressed themselves as prophets, but they were also responsible for the service of praise in the Temple. From the last sentence of the Book of Habakkuk, we may judge that he was a member of the Levitical Temple Choir, for there he requests that the music of his Psalm in chapter 3 should be played on his own stringed instruments.

The nation, Judah, faced with destruction by the mighty Chaldeans, a notoriously wicked people. Now Judah was bad, but not as bad as the Chaldeans. The people of Judah saw their plight as unfair and wanted to know what was going on. It was a question about the faithfulness of God. So Habakkuk raised his voice to God. Has God forgotten the righteous people and ceased to care? For a long time he had cried out to the Lord concerning the inequity of the land, but he had received no explanation. Habakkuk asks the Lord how long he must continue to call for protection from the evil oppressor. Can't you imagine his hoarse voice as he tries to get the Lord's attention? It isn't fair! It isn't right! Has the Lord turned a deaf ear to his own people—to allow a nation as wicked as the Chaldeans to threaten God's faithful? Habakkuk's voice must be nearly gone by the time he taunts the Lord by pointing out the gratuitous violence of the Chaldeans and God's own apparent lack of attention (Chapter 1, verse 2). Habakkuk continues by pointing out to the Lord that the law—God's own law—is "paralyzed" and there is no prospect of Israel receiving the justice it so desperately seeks. All around God's people, the faithless powers seem unabated. There is no credible prospect of Israel receiving relief from the Chaldeans. Every right concept of what is right, what is just, what is Godly is turned on its head.

Habakkuk wanted to know why things were happening as they were to the people of God. Why does God allow evil to exist among God's people, and evil and wickedness as is seen on every hand? The principles of the Law of Moses were being cast aside, for "the law is slacked and justice never goes forth" (1:1-4). The Hebrews believed in the sovereignty of God, righteous and all powerful, whose will and purpose were expressed through events in nature and in history. The problem of how evil and good continue side by side in a world controlled by a righteous God was one that was only beginning to be thought of in Habakkuk's time. If a righteous God controls the world, then how can evil exist in this world? Why, then, does God permit this evil to go unchecked in Israel? The prophet was raising a question about the righteous character of God.

The age-old problem of why the righteous suffer and the wicked prosper is still with us today. In every generation we see this problem reenacted. There are people around the world who love God, but are without warm clothing, adequate shelter, nutritious food or decent education. People who love God, but their bodies are experiencing sickness and disease. There are injustices that go unchallenged, wars that never end, crime and violence in the streets, broken homes and poverty. Generations of people who love God have asked why me? There were righteous men and women in Judah who were faithful to God and the covenant. Yet these righteous ones would suffer also at the hands of the wicked.

In spite of the terrible situation, Habakkuk expected God to answer. Like a watchman peering into the distance, Habakkuk looked expectantly for a word. And finally, God answered Habakkuk, telling him to make his vision plain to the people, to wait patiently for God's revelation, and to pay no heed to the proud people of this world, but to stand with those who live by faith (Hab. 2:2-4).

God told Habakkuk to wait, but with hope. When the

time was right, God would act. God had not forgotten them and would keep the vision of the kingdom alive. In the meantime, they were to live as God wanted, depend on God and be faithful (Hab. 2:4).

We have that same word. We know that God has acted in Christ, and God's kingdom will never be defeated. God will do for us what we need. In the meantime, let us be faithful, living as God wants us to, depending on God for what we need. When faithful Christians are down, we keep on trusting and serving God as always.

The prophet realized that God was in His holy temple working His sovereign will, and the earth must trust Him and keep silent. Habakkuk was satisfied once he understood God's long-range plan. The last chapter of Habakkuk contains a majestic hymn of praise to God. According to Habakkuk, God is alive and active even though external events seem to indicate the opposite. Ultimately, decency wins. Sometimes this does not happen immediately, but in due time right always prevails. Habakkuk must wait for full vindication, but he will do so quietly, confident in the integrity of God's power.

What is Habakkuk's message for us? We should not deny or hide our doubts, nor should we be ashamed of them. God honors and rewards anyone who sincerely seeks the truth. Habakkuk's faith was made complete when he was willing to wait for God's answer to him. Even though disaster and destruction was in his future, Habakkuk comes to realize that he can trust implicitly in his Lord. The ultimate goal or outcome of history is determined by God. Time is on God's side, for the ages belong to God in which to reveal justice and to work out God's purposes.

The Apostle Paul takes up this statement of Habakkuk and makes it the central theme of his message to the Romans:

"For I am not ashamed of the gospel; it is the power of God for salvation to everyone who has faith, to the Jew first and also to the Greek. For in it the righteousness of God is revealed through faith for faith; as it is written, 'The one who is righteous will live by faith'" (Romans 1:16-17).

The essential truth is that real life is that which is lived in union with God. That union is one of faith, trust and belief in the love and righteous character of God.

Isaiah 40:31 says, and I paraphrase, Believers who are patient and longsuffering in their faith will not be disappointed by our God. The Lord will give them an infusion of power and a new range of abilities that will surprise themselves and their adversaries. Then he concludes with that famous image of strong believers adorned with wings as strong as those of eagles, promising that the strength that comes from the Lord will allow Believers to run without becoming weary and walk forever without fainting. Re-red that lyrical passage in your Bible and savor the comfort of Isaiah's poetic words of comfort.

Questions for Reflection and Meditation

• Has my faith grown as a result of confronting my doubts?

• Am I willing to wait patiently upon the Lord?

• Has there been a time in your own life when God seemed disinterested in your plight—especially when you were threatened by an unfair employer or other oppressive person or power?

- Can I name a time when I felt God had passed me by, not rewarded my service to the kingdom? How patient or impatient was I with God then?

CHAPTER FOUR

God Has Spoken

Hebrews 1:1-4

The writer to the Hebrews declares that the divine purpose in sending Jesus among us is to raise us to the glorious dignity of children of God. The letter to the Hebrews was written to Jewish Christians who were under tremendous peer pressure, and even persecution, to leave their Christian faith and return to Judaism. This introductory chapter to Hebrews overwhelms us with spiritual facts about Christ – God's messenger. Hebrews presents the Son of God as better than the prophets and as better than the angels. This entire epistle is based on Christ as "better" than the old way, and presents many spiritual truths. Many people today experience peer pressure that would draw them away from our commitment to Christ. We, like the Hebrews, must listen carefully and think constantly on the words of the Lord and his appointed leaders. Otherwise, we are in danger of losing our way and becoming estranged from the community of believers. Take time to re-read (Hebrews, chapter 2, verse 1, and ask yourself about the strength of your attention to God's word, to wise preaching, and to the teachers who have meant the most in your walk with God. The letter to the Hebrews demonstrates how the Old Testament had been perfected and fulfilled in Christ.

The Book of Hebrews illustrates how God's final and supreme word comes to us in and through Jesus Christ. The Letter is concerned about recent converts who believed in the prophets and the angels as the only source of messages from

God. Paul stresses that Christ is superior to the prophets, the angels, the Mosaic Law and the Levitical priesthood. And he encourages new converts to listen to Jesus Christ as God's authentic and supreme messenger to the hearts of the people.

To whom did God speak in the past? How does God speak today? We all search for answers. How can we really know what God's will is for our life? What are my gifts? What meaning does the Bible have for me? How can people obtain forgiveness for their sins? God is always speaking His will to us. Some have doubted whether or not God speaks to us at all. We can have the blessed assurance that God has been, and is, in constant communication with creation. God is aware of our hopes, fears, doubts, beliefs, questions, needs, gifts, differences and experiences.

God has spoken God's love and purpose for humanity throughout the ages. There are more than 2,000 years' worth of wonderful messages delivered by the prophets. Revelations of God have been given to persons of faith, who then took the responsibility to provide spiritual guidance within their society. Before Christ, there was a limitation to the knowledge of God in creation. Humanity only knew of God's power, but not God's person. Paul's message is crystal-clear in Hebrews.

The prophets fulfilled a wonderful role in presenting God's word. But Christ is superior to the prophets because Christ is the exact image of God, and the original glory of God. Christ is the creative instrument by which God created the worlds, and the sustainer of the universe. Christ is superior to the angels in that he is eternal and superior to all created things and beings. Christ is described and declared to be the very Son of God and the object of angelic worship. The angels are described as the servants of God, as well as the servants of the heirs of salvation.

Messages from God have come to humankind in a variety of ways. God speaks to us through nature. "The heavens are telling the glory of God; and the firmament proclaims God's handiwork" (Psalm 19:1). God speaks through our conscience when we read His word, and when we worship. God speaks through us to others. We are human channels for God's message.

God speaks through the Bible. In Second Timothy, verses 16 and 17, Paul counsels that the Bible has been given to us by individuals who were alive with God's spirit, that its books are useful to us—are to be cherished by us—so that we may learn (and perhaps sometimes re-learn), so that we may correct our ways and lead our families, so that we can train our children and new brothers and sisters in Christ, and so that we may find the strength we will surely need to be prepared for all that life throws at us. As Paul writes in Romans, chapter 8, verse 31, "If God is for us, who is against us?" Many answers can be found in the pages of the Bible.

God speaks through prayer. People should go to God in prayer, if they desire intimate communication. In Matthew 7:7, the Holy One tells believers to knock on the door with the assurance that it will be opened. What doors are closed to you?

Still the various methods of revelation were inadequate to reveal God as a person. In order to do this more fully, it would take a person who was God, as well as human. So, lastly, God has spoken through his Son Jesus Christ. "Long ago God spoke to our ancestors in many and various ways by the prophets, but in these last days he has spoken to us by a Son, whom he appointed heir of all things, through whom he also created the worlds. He is the reflection of God's glory and the exact imprint of God's very being, and he sustains all things by his powerful word" (1:1-3). God sent Jesus in order to reveal God's self. Christ is the Anointed One of God, our Redeemer.

The Trinitarian view of God is the point at which Christianity separates from its sister religions. The Book of Hebrews tells us that it is God the Son who supremely reveals God's self to us. The one true personal God exists as Father, Son and Holy Spirit.

Jesus was not like God, Jesus is God – God in person, Emmanuel, God with us, The Incarnate One. To say that Jesus is the Son of God is to say that he is of the same substance as God. Jesus the Son is the same substance as God the Father. Jesus is Lord from beginning to end. "I am the Alpha and Omega," says the Lord God, who is and who was and who is to come, the Almighty" (Revelation 1:8). The Gospel of John says, "In the beginning was the Word, and the Word was with God, and the Word was God" (John 1:1). The letter to the Colossians instructs us that Jesus is the image of a God we cannot see, the premier son of creation, the one for whom all of creation awaits. It tells us that Christ is over all earthly rulers, that he in fact existed before any of this world's authorities were set in motion. Finally, it assures us that Christ is the glue that hold everything of lasting importance together (Colossians 1:15-16). Christ is the redeemer of humanity. Christ alone has provided complete and perfect redemption. "When he had made purification for sins, he sat down at the right hand of the Majesty on high" (Hebrews 1:3b).

God has spoken and continues to speak to all of creation in various ways. Let us continue to surrender to God and follow God's voice. Let us listen to one another as channels of God's message. Let us bow in worship before Christ as Redeemer and Savior. Let us continue to make him the Lord of our lives.

This letter to the Hebrews was written to prove that the new covenant in Jesus Christ is superior to the old covenant of Mount Sinai. God sent Jesus to establish the new covenant. This epistle stresses God's will, that we "believe on the name of his Son, Jesus Christ."

Christ died for our sins and was buried. He rose again the third day just as he said He would. He is alive today, affecting salvation for all who will come unto God, by him. Anyone can call on the name of the Lord, confess with your mouth and believe in your heart that God has raised him from the dead, and you will be saved. Let us hear clearly God's message of sending his son to dwell a little lower than the angels, and to die for our sins.

Questions for Reflection and Meditation

- Do I read and understand the Bible through the eyes of Christ who is the Word?

- Do I really believe in God as expressed through Jesus Christ?

- Can I think of a time when a particular Bible verse or passage seemed to come to me like a revelation—perhaps it fit a new situation or took on a new meaning?

- How do I express my appreciation for the suffering Jesus accomplished on the cross for my sake?

CHAPTER FIVE

Speak, Lord, for Your Servant Is Listening

1 Samuel 3:1-10

As we study history, we discover many women and men who have looked beyond their present to see future possibilities. Visionary people look beyond where we are to where we might be. This is also true in the life of faith. God gives some people unique insights. One example of a New Testament visionary is the Apostle Paul. He envisioned a church that included both Jews and Gentiles. A modern-day visionary, Mother Teresa, raised the awareness of the world to the plight of those who suffer, whether affluent or among the poor.

Are you seeking to know God's purpose and direction for your life, your family, your career? Do you need a vision from the Lord? Our text offers insights into the kind of faith that visionaries have that allows them to see what God has promised for God's people. God's visions come to people of authentic faith and obedient hearts. Every person is capable of experiencing a sense of calling. The call to be a disciple of Jesus Christ is a sense of realizing that "this is what I must do, this is who I am." If we retrace our steps, we might discover that all along the way we have been led to this point, and recognize God's hand in it.

Samuel in the Old Testament, and Dr. Martin Luther King Jr. in more recent times, are prime examples of people who have heard and obeyed the call of God. The Bible tells us that Samuel was a special gift from God to his mother

Hannah because of her most fervent prayer. After weaning Samuel, Hannah went to the temple and presented him to Eli, the sanctuary priest.

There must have been days when the young Samuel, probably 12 years of age by this time, wondered what his mother had gotten him into. He had spent virtually his whole childhood assisting in the temple at Shiloh, training to become a full-time servant of God. Eli's eyesight had greatly deteriorated, and he needed Samuel to wait on him. One of Samuel's many tasks was to attend to the light that burned in the temple. The light in the temple was kept burning in the darkness to remind the people of the presence of God. Samuel was doing basically the same kind of thing that our acolytes do today. Our acolytes do a wonderful service for Pulaski Heights United Methodist Church, lighting and maintaining the candles during worship, to remind us of God's presence.

The word of the Lord was rare in those days; visions were not widespread. Eli and his sons were the leaders of the people. But Eli's sons were evil. Eli knew of the sins of his sons and did nothing to stop them. The Bible tells us they were scoundrels who cared nothing for the Lord. The people were lost because their leaders were lost. They had no guidance or direction in their lives.

One faithful night, God called Samuel as he slept in the temple of the Lord, where the Ark of God was. The word of the Lord had not yet been revealed to him, so Samuel assumed that it was Eli calling him because they were the only two persons present. "Samuel! Samuel!" He runs to Eli, but is quickly sent back to bed very confused. Once again the voice came, "Samuel!" Again Samuel ran to Eli, and Eli told him to lie down. After a third call from God, Eli, the wise and obedient chief priest who had become dull and negligent, finally realizes that God is calling Samuel.

Samuel's mentor Eli gives him three good things to do. "Go, lie down; and if he calls you, you shall say, 'Speak, Lord, for your servant is listening'" (v. 9). Eli's advice to "lie down" is a way of saying relax and trust God. Samuel is then instructed to listen with his ears and all his senses, and "if he calls you again," speak up.

Eli knew that God wanted an answer. God waits for us to respond, to question, and even challenge the divine word that comes to us. God has never been afraid of a little discussion or debate. When was the last time you talked back to God?

So once again God called Samuel and he responded, "Speak, Lord, for your servant is listening." The word, the vision, came when Samuel was home lying down in his own bed. The word of the Lord first revealed to Samuel the destruction of Eli's house and the revelation that Samuel would replace Eli. Samuel became a great prophet, priest, judge and a leader of God's people.

First Samuel 3:19-20says that Samuel grew up in a close relationship with the Lord, that the Lord provided him visions and the word to express those visions. It tells us that Samuel's reputation as one close to the Lord was well known. The first encounter Samuel had with God was his conversion experience, as well as his call as a prophet. The Book of Deuteronomy 18:15-22 tells us how to distinguish a true prophet from a false one. A true prophet is one who speaks in a way that calls upon humanity to follow and obey God. A true prophet is one whose words come to pass. Everything Samuel says will happen, does happen. And every Israelite realizes that God's hand is upon Samuel and that he speaks the word of the Lord.

The powerful leadership of the Rev. Dr. Martin Luther

King Jr. responded to God and to the needs of our time. His message of justice and inclusion changed our own country and the way we live forever. Through the civil rights movement, and Dr. King, the vision of God's future was made manifest and many people were moved into action.

Dr. King loved to tell his story. He did not have personal plans to become a national civil rights leader. Born in Atlanta, Georgia, he entered nearby Morehouse College at age 15 and graduated with a bachelor's degree in sociology in 1948. At the age of 18, Dr. King was ordained as a Baptist minister. After graduating with honors from Crozer Theological Seminary in Pennsylvania in 1951, he went to Boston University where he earned a doctoral degree in systematic theology in 1955.

Dr. King really wanted a quiet life as a pastor, professor, possibly president of Morehouse College or a university someday. As a young pastor he was thrust into the forefront of the Montgomery bus boycott. He arrived home late one night, tired and frightened. The phone rang and an angry voice on the other end said, "We're gonna get you!" Dr. King stood in his kitchen, frozen in fear. He wanted to call Daddy King for reassurance and advice, but Daddy King wasn't there. Then he said it was like a voice. "Martin, you do what's right. You stand up for justice. You be my drum major for righteousness. I'll be with you." Dr. King heard his name called. He knew what God wanted him to do and say. Because Dr. King listened and responded to God, his life and the world were forever changed.

On August 28, 1963, at the March on Washington, a massive protest for jobs and civil rights, Dr. King delivered the keynote address. His memorable "I Have a Dream" speech expressed the hopes of the civil rights movement and created the political momentum, along with the Birmingham demonstrations, that resulted in the Civil Rights Act of 1964. This act prohibited segregation in public accommodations, as well as discrimination in education and employment. As a result of Dr. King's effectiveness as a leader of the American civil rights movement and his highly visible moral stance, he was awarded the 1964 Nobel Prize for peace.

Eli's advice to Samuel was for him to respond, "Speak, Lord, for your servant is listening." Dr. King said: "I have a dream that one day this nation will rise up and live out the true meaning of its creed: 'We hold these truths to be self-evident, that all men are created equal.'... I have a dream that my four little children will one day live in a nation where they will not be judged by the color of their skin but by the content of their character."

Dr. King, in his sermon titled "The Drum Major Instinct," said, "... everybody can be great, because everybody can serve. You don't have to have a college degree to serve. You don't have to make your subject and your verb agree to serve. You don't have to know about Plato and Aristotle to serve ... You only need a heart full of grace, a soul generated by love. And you can be that servant."

Dr. King concluded this sermon by quoting a song: "If I can help somebody as I pass along, if I can cheer somebody with a word or song, then my living will not be in vain. If I can do my duty as a Christian ought, if I can bring salvation to a world once wrought, if I can spread the message as the master taught, then my living will not be in vain."

Without a vision of God's will for us we are lost. The scripture says that Samuel lived in a time in which the word of the Lord was rare, but God did not leave them visionless. Some may feel that the word of God is rare in our time. God is calling people to be servants to one another, prophets and leaders. God is calling the young and older persons alike. And we all need one another to help us hear God's directions. God is calling all of his people into ministry, because we are all his children.

Questions for Reflection and Meditation

• Have I ever witnessed someone acting as an inspired visionary for God? If so, how did I respond at the time? How do I feel now about my response at that time?

• Does God, the Holy Spirit, speak to me?

• When have I felt that "Drum Major Instinct?" How did I act on it?   How did I feel afterward?

• Do I listen to God? Daily...or only on certain occasions?

CHAPTER SIX

Guided By the Spirit

Acts 4:5-12

Prayer: Grant, O God, that today and every time we come before you in worship and prayer, we may be vividly aware of your presence among us. May we sense your power, protection and love as revealed through Jesus Christ our Lord. Amen.

The Third Sunday of Easter, in the United Methodist Church, is Festival of the Christian Home Sunday. The purpose of this observance is to focus attention on families in our congregations, the community and the world. Most families have rules, guidelines and values to increase their quality of life, and to lead them through the complexities and dynamics of living within community.

Because of our human free will, one thing is certain about life, there are many decisions to make each day. The Christian Church teaches that the Spirit of Christ, "The Holy Spirit," is available to each and everyone, and is able to assist in any decision making process. There is nothing more refreshing than to encounter or experience a person, family, mother, father, community or student that is guided and "filled with the Holy Spirit" of God. People who are "guided by the Spirit" are additional assets within community life.

Peter and John were two of Jesus' apostles who were guided by, and filled with, the Spirit of God. One day Peter and John were going up to the temple for prayer. They stopped and healed a lame beggar at the gate of the temple, which was called the beautiful gate. They proclaimed to the astonished crowd that it was the work of their God, the God who had raised Jesus from the dead. The temple authorities arrested them, and the next day Peter and John were brought before the Sanhedrin Council, or court, for a hearing.

Peter and John were just being obedient to the Great Commission. Jesus instructed his disciples to make disciples of all peoples, to baptize all nations in the name of the Father, Son and Holy Spirit. Jesus told them to teach all peoples to obey God's commandments. He assured His followers that He would be with them without fail throughout their days (Matthew 28:19-20). As it is recorded in Matthew chapter 10, verses 7 and 8, He instructed them to persevere in spreading the Good News, to cure those who were ill, to relieve the worst of conditions—even leprosy, to rid sufferers of demons and even to raise the dead.

Peter and John were simply going around talking to people about the Lord Jesus. They were "filled with the Holy Spirit," which means they were aware of Jesus' indwelling presence and were committed fully to his guidance and leadership. They were consciously dependent on the Holy Spirit for wisdom, knowledge and spiritual vitality, which is necessary for doing God's work. After being arrested for doing the work of the Holy Spirit, Peter and John were asked (v. 7b), "By what power or by what name do you do this miracle of healing?"

According to the Gospels, Jesus had warned his disciples that they would be brought before Jewish religious authorities and interrogated for doing God's work. Jesus instructed them not to be anxious about how they would react or what they would say. He told them that the Holy Spirit would be there to provide the right words, and to put those words in their mouths so they need not worry (Matthew 10:19-20). Luke says the same thing: do not fret about what to say when you are dragged before authorities; the Hold Spirit will be there at the very moment of your distress to provide exactly the right words (Luke 12:11-12).

This was the same reassurance Yahweh had given Moses, "Now go, and I will be with your mouth and teach you what you are to speak" (Exodus 4:12).

So, as Peter stands before the Sanhedrin Council, which is the supreme court of Israel, consisting of 71 of the most wealthy, powerful, educated and cultured Jewish leaders of the time, verse 8 tells us that Peter is "filled with the Holy Spirit." The boldness of Peter and John surely was visible to the Sanhedrin.

Peter, the natural spokesperson, explains the miracle of healing the crippled man at the beautiful gate of the temple, and presents a disturbing contrast to the council. It is the power of Jesus Christ of Nazareth, the man whom you crucified, but whom God has raised from the dead. Peter, indirectly, tells the Jewish authorities that they actually had a hand in this miracle. Peter, "guided by the Holy Spirit," continues to inform the court by quoting Psalm 118:22 with a personal emphasis: "The stone that was rejected by you, the builders; it has become the cornerstone." Peter expressed the divine reversal that had taken place at Easter, through their rejection, God had responded with exaltation.

The Jewish leaders acted exactly as they had with Jesus. They asked Peter and John, the same question they had asked Jesus. In verse 7b, the question that is on everyone's mind was asked: by whose order or power or in whose name was this done? Peter's response paralyzed the religious leaders. The Sanhedrin Council thought they were the only ones who could speak for God. They had been shaped and blinded by historical experiences.

The ancient Jews had received a series of dramatic revelations of the nature of God during the time of Moses. God had repeatedly shown them, in awesome and unmistakable ways, his grace, love and mercy. God continued to occasionally speak to them through prophets and other inspired teachers. The Jewish leaders had dutifully written down God's revelations to them, and entrusted these writing to a special group of men, called priests, to pass on to future generations.

God's special outpourings of grace and revelations to the Jews gradually became fewer and fewer, until four centuries prior to the time of Jesus, recorded revelations had ceased altogether. Previous revelations of God to the Jews became more and more precious. As their value increased, the Jewish priests who copied and protected the written record of these former revelations gained increased authority and power. The priests and scribes were the only ones who handled these rare and sacred materials. By the time of Jesus, the temple priests of Jerusalem and the scribes managed the sacred word of God. God's revelations had become a limited resource in the hands of the high Jewish religious authorities to present and interpret.

Then, a man named Jesus, from Nazareth, came along claiming that God's revelations to the Jews had not ceased, and that he was a new revelation of God, not only for the Jews, but for all humanity. Jesus shared the Good News with all people, and many of the people responded with joy. The leadership of the time responded to Jesus by crucifying him on a wooden cross.

A few months later, men calling themselves apostles, find themselves standing where Jesus stood because they had healed a crippled man while going to the temple. They had publicly proclaimed that God was freely available to

Jews and Gentiles. They also announced with great joy that God had raised from the dead the man named Jesus, who had been killed for the same crime.

While filled with the Holy Spirit, verse 9 tells us that Peter says to that powerful assembly, and I paraphrase, "Authorities, you powerful men and elders, if anyone questions the benevolent deed of compassion and love that has been done among us today to one who suffered in sickness, if anyone asks of you how this man was relieved and made well, let me tell you now and let you reply to any who ask—to all the people of Israel—that this man is stands here in your sight by power of and in the name of Jesus of Nazareth, the Christ." Peter then explicitly places salvation in Christ, telling the people that no other authority can provide the salvation which all people seek (Acts 4:12).

Out of this simple miracle story there arises proclamation of the Easter faith. Peter and John, "uneducated, common men" (v. 13), pointed out to the religious authorities the connection between "a good deed done to a crippled man" and the work of God in which they themselves had participated.

Miracles happen when we are guided by the Holy Spirit. Only Christ can continue to heal our land, save our families and give us sure instructions for faithful living. Let us pray that God will overwhelm our mothers, our fathers, our families, our graduates, our community and the world with the wonders of the Holy Spirit. Let us continue to share the good news of God's love with those around us.

Questions for Reflection and Meditation

- Is the Holy Spirit in control of my life?

- When have you felt like "the cornerstone that was rejected?" How did you respond to that rejection?

- Am I free to follow the leading of the Holy Spirit?

- Do I secretly desire to sit in a position of temporal power (or do I in fact sit in power) in a very self-satisfying way that keeps my spirit from accepting God's power over my life?

CHAPTER SEVEN

I Believe in Jesus of Nazareth

Mark 6:1-13

I believe that Jesus was born in Bethlehem and was reared in Nazareth. I also believe that Jesus was fully human and fully divine. Philippians 2:5c-8 assures me that Jesus Christ, while he was in fact God, did not hide behind divinity but, instead became like a slave—the lowest of the lowly—among the humans into whose community he was born. In human form, it says, he was unimaginably humble and obedient—even to the extremity of death and then even to death on a cross.

The Christian conviction is really not, "I believe in Jesus Christ," but rather, "I believe that Jesus is the Christ." The Christian conviction is that in Jesus of Nazareth, God sent the Messiah. Jesus is not an idea or a symbol, but a person living under the conditions of time and relationships. I believe in Jesus the Christ, or Messiah, someone who saves, delivers, heals and brings relief to life's many situations. Jesus the person grew up in a community of real people who knew him as the son of a local carpenter. Can you imagine the difficulty that people of Nazareth and vicinity has accepting that this local man suddenly acquired a following, that he was reputed to heal sick people and even raise the dead? If it is difficult for much of today's world to accept the divinity of Jesus, how much more difficult must it have been for those who had watched him grow up among them—or in that sleepy village down the lane—when his ministry shook the region?

I believe that our great salvation includes more than the salvation of our soul, which is the free gift of God when we put faith and trust in Jesus Christ as Lord and Savior. It includes more than a new body and a heavenly home, which our Lord is preparing for those who love him. I believe that my salvation also involves living the heavenly way of life here and now in the power of the risen and living Lord.

I believe that Jesus was and is the Master Teacher who came from God to give wisdom to believers, and that Jesus is the way to the highest possible human happiness. Through his teachings our Lord came to correct us, to inform us and to change our lives. He wants to instruct our minds, stir our emotions and affect our will as we make decisions that will be pleasing to God. To be a true follower of Jesus Christ, we let his teachings determine our attitudes, actions and ambitions. I believe that "If you confess with your lips that Jesus is Lord, and believe in your heart that God raised him from the dead, you will be saved" (Romans 10:9).

The words "Jesus of Nazareth" suggest that the Messiah had a boyhood home in this world, but the text makes it plain that his own people rejected him. Mark tells us that Jesus went back home to minister in Nazareth. The fact that his disciples went with him indicates that this was a preaching mission and not just a nostalgic homecoming. Mark 6 is all about Jesus of Nazareth in Nazareth. The issue in Mark is how the people who new Jesus best responded to him.

Jesus went home on the Sabbath and taught in the synagogue, and those who heard him were offended. Jesus' friends and family assumed that he would sit and smile quietly, giving the family an opportunity to worship together again. But on this day, Jesus did not come to listen and learn, but to teach and admonish. Jesus' hearers were astonished, and the people were saying such things as: "Who does he think he is? He's no better than we are. Is not this the carpenter, the son of Mary and brother of James and Joseph and Judas and Simon, and are not his sisters here with us? And they took offense at him" (Mark 6:3). There is always someone who remembers us growing up, and sometimes no matter what we do in life, they are not impressed.

In response to this hostile reception, Jesus gave us the line that has ever since been applied to those who go back home and find the hometown folks unimpressed. "Prophets are not without honor, except in their hometown, and among their own kin and in their own house" (Mark 6:4). He was telling them, in the words of a contemporary expression, "Familiarity breeds contempt."

This hometown visit followed a series of mighty miracles performed by Jesus: calming the storm, healing the Gerasene demoniac, restoring a little girl to life and healing a woman with a hemorrhage. And then Jesus went home, and a crowd of people experienced his deeds and wonders and his prophetic preaching. But the crowd remembers that Jesus is one of the locals, one of them, and so they do not believe in Jesus. No one was impressed, and Jesus was amazed at their unbelief.

So, how did Jesus respond to this failure, this rejection by those who knew him so well? He immediately sent his disciples to teach and heal. Jesus then told them what to do if they ever went to a place that would not receive them. "If any place will not welcome you and they refuse to hear you, as you leave, shake off the dust that is on your feet as a testimony against them" (Mark 6:11). In other words, do not let the failure continue to cling to your heels. Go on with life, with the next challenge.

Jesus' experience with his family and friends back

home can be instructive for us today. For those of us who are intentionally trying to live close to Jesus, there are good examples for us here.

First, I believe that Jesus wants us to minister and to witness to our family and friends, but it can be very difficult. Jesus tried to do it and was not too successful. There were some who were healed. Jesus' example here encourages us to share the faith with even our friends and family. Tell your family and friends why you love them. Tell them about your love for Jesus and your desire for them to know him also. Tell them how you want them to be the best they can be. Reach out and touch the heart of someone who is hurting by sharing your faith in Christ. We can be at least as enthusiastic about our faith as we are about our wonderful recreational activities and our loved ones.

Jesus shared the faith with those who meant the most to him. He knew that His responsibility was to plant the seed. Some day it could blossom into full faith. As sharers of the faith, we should never let human barriers or risks deter us. In Jesus' situation, some were healed and that was enough. Our responsibility is to go where we are called, and sent.

Second, I believe that we must be careful that we do not come too close for comfort and dismiss the claims of Christianity by analyzing away the faith, nor should we produce quick and easy answers. Jesus' listeners had analyzed the situation and decided that no good could come out of their little town of Nazareth. Jesus just wasn't what they had in mind for a Messiah. He was too ordinary for anyone to really expect extraordinary miracles from him.

The danger for faithful Christians is that we may be too close to Jesus for comfort. We may become relaxed or even snobbish at times. Some may believe that we are the ones who define the categories in which the Holy Spirit operates. Just because we've never done it that way before doesn't mean that God doesn't want to do it that way now. I believe that we have to be ready for fresh revelations, for new winds, for different directions, for exciting futures in our own lives and in our own church's life.

Our world loves a good success story, but most of us have experienced perceived failure and weaknesses at times. For that reason we can take heart when we receive the Holy Sacrament. I believe that it is the sacrament that makes it possible for us to shake from our feet the dust of failure and move on toward life's next challenge. I believe that it is Holy Communion that makes it possible for us to look to the new beginnings, the new possibilities that Christ offers.

When we receive the Eucharist, if we know or have known any failure in our lives, let the sacrament be the moment of a new beginning. For we are people who are nourished by the heavenly food of one who looked beyond the disappointment of failure to the hope of new beginnings. Thus we are not immobilized by failure, but energized by possibility. So whatever the perceived failure – morality, relationships, commitment, hope or vision – shake off the dust from your feet and go out into a new future. You will find beside you Our Lord Jesus, the Messiah.

Questions for Reflection and Meditation

- Do I live my witness in everyday life and in all circumstances?

- Am I comfortable in my faith response?

- Have I ever reacted to the Church with the impulse to deny a call for participation, generosity or faith, questioning why the established ways of worship, service or stewardship are being usurped?

- When have I been too comfortable in my faith? How did I overcome that excess of pride and return to a vital faith?

CHAPTER EIGHT

I Believe in the Ministry of All Christians

2 Corinthians 5:17-21

Prayer: Almighty God, you began your creation anew in your Son Jesus, not counting our sins against us but reconciling us and granting to us the ministry of reconciliation. We pray for the power of your Holy Spirit, that we may confidently and lovingly obey you as your ambassadors, imploring all people to be reconciled to you and spreading the good news of your new creation to the world you love. In Jesus' name we pray. Amen.

I believe in the ministry of all Christians that is shaped by the teachings of Jesus. Christian ministry is the expression of the mind and mission of Christ, through a community of Christians that demonstrates a life of devotion, witness, gratitude, service, celebration and discipleship.

I believe that every Christian is gifted and called by God to servant ministries and servant leadership. I believe that the form of ministry for each Christian is "… diverse in locale, in interest and denominational accent, yet always catholic (universal) in spirit and outreach" (UMC Discipline, Sec. 104, 1996).

I believe that lay ministry is essential to the mission and ministry of congregations, because lay ministries produce Christian disciples. The United Methodist Church recognizes laypersons as well as ordained persons as being gifted and called by God to provide leadership in the Church.

These gifts are revealed through Christ who came not to be served but to serve (Mark 10:45), and to give his life for the world. The Holy Spirit has been given to every believer. And all Christians have been given the ministry of reconciliation. The ministry of laity and clergy, all Christians, is complementary. No ministry is more important than another, because there is only one ministry in Christ. There are diverse gifts, and evidences of God's grace in the body of Christ, when we express the will of God in practical daily living.

Ephesians 4:4-7 says that, in Christ, there is "one body" and "one Spirit." Just as each believer is personally called, our world is governed by "one Lord, one faith, one baptism." This passage assures us that there is one God who is over all creation and in fact is in all creation. It goes on to assure us that each believer receives a free gift of grace because of Christ.

God has not set out merely to improve us, to alter us slightly, or even to reform us. He intends to remake us. We are told plainly that, once each of us in Christ—surrendered to Him—that person is an entirely new creation. Christians are evidence that God's power turns out new creatures, creates fresh life from God's very hands. Paul's words are very clear: he writes that our old self disappears, is forever gone. The believer is a new creation, unchained from the behaviors, prejudices and limitations of poor spirit that likely characterized the person prior to conversion. So, God's new creation will be newer tomorrow than it is today, and all this is from God.

When we accept the gift of God to make us all new, we find reconciliation and peace. In Christ we participate in a whole new reconciled reality. It is not that the old is lost, but the old is united in reconciliation and redemption with the Christian community, and thus made new. The love of Christ controls us, and that changes everything about how we look at others, and live with them. When we look from God's point of view, or a Divine perspective, we recognize that Christ suffered and died for all people, and we can not devalue any person. God has placed a high value on all humanity. No one person is more or less than another. God has taken the initiative through Christ to love and care for us.

Christ's way of dealing with sin is not to excuse it, which would mean sin is not important, but Christ forgives sin. Paul writes, "not counting their trespasses against them." As Paul says in verse 21, "For our sake he made him to be sin who knew no sin, so that in him we might become the righteousness of God."

I believe that God is opposed to our sin, but that God also fixes it for us so we no longer are trapped, boxed in, held back, limited by yesterday's mistakes. God does not stand away from us, but enters our lives through Christ. When all things become new, all of the new convert's choices become more potent and full of possibilities for expression of the Spirit of Christ and entirely empowered by the new gifts present in the believer. In Christ, each of us has a new relationship with God. We are no longer condemned sinners, but now justified. The believer—each one of us— is welcomed into the family of fellowship with God. This is not a passive welcoming, but an inauguration into new powers—new gifts—granted by God's grace so that each believer can exercise the Spirit of Christ in ministry. This is part of what it means when we say that a place is being prepared for us in Heaven, and we have been promised an eternity with God.

Christians play a wonderful role in God's plan for

bringing the world to God's self. Because God reconciled us to God's very self, we can also help others to be reconciled to God. In so many ways we are called to take the place of Christ, to be Christ, for others around us. God is calling us to bring the love and presence of Christ to those who are hurting and in need of care and support as they go through life's many challenges.

The New Testament describes the mystery of God's reconciling act in Jesus in many ways: a shepherd's life given for his sheep, atonement by a priest, victory over the powers of evil, the sacrifice of a lamb, the ransom of a slave, the payment of a debt. All these are ways the New Testament witnesses to the belief and the experience of our being made right with God again.

I believe that just as Christ assumed our place in this world, now Christ commands us to take His place in this world. I believe that our place in the Kingdom—and, for now, in this world—is freely given to us because of Jesus and his Father. The Lord has given us a ministry of absolute reconciliation through Jesus Christ (2 Cor. 5:18). God has committed to us the message of reconciliation, which is the Gospel of Jesus Christ. We are Christ's ambassadors. There is nothing passive about our reconciliation with the Lord; we are given new gifts and expected to grow into them, to employ them in ministry. God sends his message to others through us. How can we bear that message unless we are absolutely reconciled ourselves? (2 Cor. 5:20). We have the authority and responsibility as God's ambassadors on earth to love, care for, confront, forgive and reconcile others to God and to one another.

As ambassadors for Christ, with great responsibility and authority, we are focused on what Christ tells us is important. We reach out to everyone, whether we feel like it or not, even to people who are quite different from ourselves, because of Christ's passion. Our job, in our own ways, and in our own words, is to communicate to others that God loves humanity and forgives. God has made many persons friends through Christ, and there are many people today who are in need of a caring friend like us.

Many are hospitalized and fighting illness, some are homebound. Some are locked into physical prisons, and others suffer in emotional prisons. Some are enduring crushing grief for a deceased loved one, suffering through divorce, facing a pregnancy with fear, or may have lost a job. Others are victims of domestic violence and troubled families. Many people are lonely and hurting around us.

We have many people at Pulaski Heights United Methodist Church who are on the front lines of lay caring ministries, ministering to these persons. The Society of St. Stephen members, Cancer Friends, Grief Support members, Parkinson's support members, divorce recovery members, Helping Hands Respite Care, United Methodist Women Circles, Sunday school classes, the Mission Board, trained Stephen Ministers and many other church groups.

They go as God's ambassadors, with full authority to love others, to pray for others, and to forgive others for God. How else will the hurting people in our community and world know that God loves them.

The United Methodist Church states that:

"We are called together for worship and fellowship and for the up building of the Christian community. We advocate and work for the unity of the Christian church. We call persons into discipleship ... As servants of Christ we are sent into the world to engage in the struggle for justice and reconciliation. We seek to reveal the love of God for men, women and children of all ethnic, racial, cultural and national backgrounds and to demonstrate the healing power of the gospel with those who suffer" (UMC Discipline, Sec. 103, 1996).

Questions for Reflection and Meditation

• What gifts of the spirit has God given me?   What do my spiritual gifts say about what God expects of me?

• Have I employed one gift and ignored another? If so, what is holding me back from exercising the ignored gift(s)?

• What have I done this week to build up the body of believers?

• Have I been open to a total transformation by the Holy Spirit, or have I tried to control God's efforts to totally remake me?

• What have I done recently to encourage a fellow Christian to embrace her/his gifts?   Have I affirmed others when they have used their gift(s) effectively?

CHAPTER NINE

Remember Your Baptism and Be Thankful

Luke 3:15-17, 21-22

Each year, on the first Sunday after the Epiphany, we commemorate the coming of the Magi to visit the baby Jesus. We also remember the baptism of Jesus. The seven-week season after the Epiphany is observed from the first Sunday after January 6 (the Twelfth Day of Christmas) until Ash Wednesday.

Epiphany is the appearance or sudden manifestation of God, or a sudden manifestation or perception of the essential nature or meaning of something. The season of Epiphany is the time we renew our claim of Jesus as our personal Savior. We open our hearts and let Jesus come in all over again, and we are refreshed and renewed. During Epiphany we focus on ways that Jesus is revealed or made known as the Savior of the world. Epiphany begins with a reminder that you are sent into the world through your baptism to share the good news of Christ with others.

This is a season of excitement, of unveiling. No experience in Epiphany is more filled with this sense of excitement than the remembrance of the baptism of Jesus, and the remembrance of our own baptism.

We have just completed the celebration of Christmas, the birth of the Christ Child. The baby Jesus was announced by angels, visited by wise men and worshiped. Prophets told us that this child was going to save God's people, and King Herod felt threatened, and wanted this child killed. The baby Jesus is then taken into hiding to grow and develop. Then the biblical accounts of Jesus' life are silent for the next 30 years, except for the account of Jesus at the age of 12, visiting the Jerusalem Temple for three days. After 30 years of no public appearance of the Christ child, perhaps many who knew of him began to think of him as just another man, a carpenter born to a carpenter—albeit perhaps under a cloud of whispers: did some say his mother was visited by a spirit? Still others—those whose hearts had been touched in some inexplicable way— were filled with expectation. People would stand along the Jordan River watching the eccentric John the Baptist, and questioning in their hearts whether he was the Savior King who would restore their nation. John the Baptist, Jesus' second cousin had appeared out in the wilderness preaching and baptizing people. He drew great crowds from Jerusalem and from the whole Judean countryside, preaching a baptism of repentance for the forgiveness of sins, because "the people were filled with expectation" (v. 15a).

John spent his entire ministry pointing to Christ as the Messiah, He said, "I baptize you with water; but one who is more powerful than I is coming; I am not worthy to untie the thong of his sandals. He will baptize you with the Holy Spirit and with fire" (Luke 3:16). John's baptism brought people to faith and forgiveness. And he foretold the day of Pentecost when Jesus, risen from the grave, would pour out the Holy Spirit on his disciples.

John the Baptist's message also included the separation of believers from unbelievers. In Luke, chapter 3, verse 17 we read of John comparing Christ's discernment to a "winnowing fork" employed by the threshing crew, perhaps by the wise and experienced leader of that crew who knows just how to separate the valuable crop into one pile, while sorting out all of the useless chaff—the stalks, the hulls—into another pile. On that passage, John warns his audience that unlike the wheat, which will be carefully gathered and taken to his granary, the chaff will go straight to the rubbish heap, where he says it will be torched "with unquenchable fire." In Jesus' day, and in certain places today, it was common for people to produce their own bread. After growing the grain, the stalks were walked on by oxen on the threshing floor. Then a fork was used to remove the straw, and it was thrown into the air so the wind could blow the chaff, or husk, aside so the grain could be used. The remaining chaff was burned.

One day as John the Baptist was preaching and baptizing in the Jordan River, Jesus comes to be baptized by him. John would have prevented Jesus, saying, "I need to be baptized by you, and do you come to me?" But Jesus answered him, "Let it be so now; for it is proper for us in this way to fulfill all righteousness." Then John consented to baptize Jesus (Matthew 3:14-15). This event begins the ministry of Jesus.

Luke tells us that as Jesus prayed during his baptism, the heavens opened and he was anointed by the Holy Spirit, as it descended on him in the form of a dove. Then a voice came from heaven saying, "You are my Son, the beloved; with you I am well pleased" (Luke 3:22). Throughout the centuries, artists have been compelled to paint their interpretations of this scene. Have you imagined it in your own mind? Whatever visual details your imagination supplies—whether they are historically accurate or not—it was on that day and in that place that Jesus was publicly declared the Christ. On that day, the one God sent to save humanity by suffering in our place, accepted his task in this world. How did God respond? We are told that a voice from Heaven told those present that God was pleased. From that day forward, Jesus took up the task for which he was sent to this world. He became "the Christ," "the Messiah," "The Anointed One." The baptism of Jesus also reveals the Holy Trinity. Jesus the Eternal Son stood in the flesh being baptized, the Holy Spirit descended in the form of a dove, and God's voice was heard from heaven. Eternal Son, Holy Spirit, and God's voice – the Trinity.

The Gospel of Luke emphasizes the role of the Holy Spirit in the mission of Jesus (Luke 1:35; 3:22). The Book of Acts focuses on the role of the Holy Spirit in the life of the church, as the Body of Christ. Our participation in the fulfilling of the commission of the church depends on the power of the Holy Spirit being active in our lives (Acts 1:7).

Do you remember your baptism? Do you think that your baptism was as exciting as Jesus' baptism? You may not remember your actual baptism if you were baptized as an infant, as Methodist believe and often do, and that is fine. Do you remember the first time you realized that God was intimately involved in your life? Do you remember the first time you felt God's grace and realized that your sins were forgiven, and that God loved you, just as you were.

Jesus sends the Holy Spirit to guide and strengthen our lives and the lives of all that believe in Him and are baptized in his name. The Holy Spirit is God's promise of strength and power to enable us to live in these difficult days. It guides and strengthens us in our times of testing, through the trials and troubles of this world. All we have to do is open our hearts.

The baptism of Jesus was different from our baptism because Jesus did not need to be washed clean from any sins. Jesus was sinless, and so John the Baptist asked Jesus if his baptism was necessary. Jesus replied, "It is proper for us to do this to fulfill all righteousness." Jesus was baptized because it was what God demands of sinners, and Jesus wanted to fulfill every righteous act that God required of the people that he came to save.

Our baptism is evidence of God working in our lives and commissioning us to be all that God wants us to be. We are disciples of reconciliation and healing in the world. Baptism is the beginning of our preparation to grow in faith and serve others. Baptism is God entering our lives and embracing us as His children. At baptism, God makes the claim, "you are mine, and with you I am well pleased!" No matter what we do, God is working in our lives. From infant baptism through adulthood, baptism was, and is, the start of our formal and personal relationship with God.

And believe it or not, our baptism was just as powerful as Jesus' baptism. Whether we recall the exact event or not, the Holy Spirit was poured out on us at our baptism. We were accepted by God as his daughters and sons through the water and Spirit. Our faith was formed and strengthened. We can renew our baptism by remembering how God has claimed us and nurtured us in the faith. God loves us so much—today, every day—that he gave his one and only Son in fair exchange for our sins, that we might be assured—in advance—of eternal life " (John 3:16). The Epiphany and baptism of Jesus remind us that God has not forgotten us or forsaken the world.

The United Methodist Church's Baptismal Covenant IV says, "Remember your baptism, and be thankful. The Holy Spirit work within you, that having been born through water and the Spirit, you may live as faithful disciples of Jesus Christ."

Questions for Reflection and Meditation

• Do I remember my own baptism? How does my baptism affect my daily life? If it has little or no effect, what would I consider doing to change that?

• Can I share the story of my baptism with others? What do I feel when I contemplate telling my own baptism story?

• How do I feel when reading of Christ's baptism? Does that story have meaning in my spiritual life? Have I ever taken time to contemplate what I would have felt if I had been among the crowd that day?

CHAPTER TEN

The Grace Within Table Fellowship

1 Corinthians 11:23-26

Prayer: Almighty God, your Son, on the night before he suffered, instituted the Sacrament of his Body and Blood: Mercifully, grant that we may receive it thankfully in the precious name of Jesus Christ our Lord, who lives and reigns with you and the Holy Spirit, one God, forever and ever. Amen.

When we celebrate the Lord's Supper, we are participating in an element of Christian worship that has been observed since the founding of the church, and was instituted by Jesus Christ Himself.

The Lord's Supper or Holy Communion is the last meal Jesus shared with his disciples prior to his death. Whether this meal was actually before or during Passover, it should still be viewed in the context of the table fellowship that was a distinctive feature of Jesus' ministry. Jesus loved table fellowship and conversation. "The grace within table fellowship" can be experienced in the open general invitation to the Lord's Table, in the forgiveness of our sins through the passion of Jesus, in the fellowship with Christ and His Body of Believers, and in the promised blessed hope of eternal life.

Christians have several traditions, practices and names associated with this sacrament. Some traditions would refer to it as a Mystery, the Mass, the Eucharist or Thanksgiving.

Protestant churches usually call this service the Lord's Supper, or the Lord's Table, or the sacrament of Holy Communion.

We believe that Holy Communion is a sacrament of the church that brings us into the presence of God. As United Methodists, we believe that the Lord is present at this meal in a special way. While the elements of bread and wine are only symbols, they are symbols of the opportunity to experience the grace within table fellowship. When Jesus said that we were to eat of His flesh and drink of His blood, He meant that we could by faith enter into a living relationship and communion with Him and the entire Body of Christ. So when you prepare to celebrate Holy Communion, ask God to give you a fresh appreciation for this time of worship and a fresh awareness of His presence in our midst.

The words "after supper," quoted by Paul, in 1 Corinthians 11:23-25 indicate that the Lord's Supper was originally a full meal, introduced by the blessing and breaking of the bread and concluded by the blessing and passing of the cup. Today, however, it is widely assumed that by the time 1 Corinthians was written the bread and cup were taken together at the end of the common meal. They were taken as a special sacramental act to remember the life, death and resurrection of Jesus.

In the New Testament, Christian fellowship was the bond among believers that was created by their common sharing and confession that Jesus is Lord. They gathered as a community at the Lord's Supper, ate from the one loaf of bread and shared the one cup, symbolizing many individuals becoming one Body in Christ. They were a body of Christians having a common faith and discipline. Fellowship with Christ meant that believers shared in his death and experienced the new life that corresponds with his resurrection.

Koinonia is the Greek word for participating in Christian fellowship and communion. Koinonia defines the relationships experienced by Christians with God, Jesus Christ, the Holy Spirit and among themselves in the early church and until this day.

The apostles teaching inspired a devoted fellowship, marked by service to others, the breaking of bread in a ritual feast that symbolized Christ's sacrifice for them, and they prayed continually for each other. These practices resulted in large numbers being saved" (Acts 2:42, 47).

"God is faithful; by him you were called into the fellowship of his Son, Jesus Christ our Lord" (1 Corinthians 1:9).

First Corinthians 13:13 counsels believers to live by faith, with hope and love. Above all, we are to live in constant gratitude and practice love.

The Lord's Supper is primarily a corporate and communal act of worship. It is understood as a spiritual family feast and community gathering. Therefore, we believe that everyone is invited and welcome to come to the table, regardless of age, gender or race. And everyone is offered forgiveness of their sins in Jesus' name.

The guest list for those invited to Holy Communion is extremely inclusive. "Christ our Lord invites to his table all who love him, and who earnestly repent of their sin and seek to live in peace with one another." So who is Christ including in this worldwide invitation? Children, youth, adults, the aging, the homeless, the oppressed, those who are abused, the poor and extremely poor, middle class, wealthy, black, white, yellow and brown. The physically, emotionally, mentally and generally challenged. The illiterate, poorly educated, educated, well-educated, criminals, moral and immoral, and exemplary people. "Christ invites all who love him, and who earnestly repent of their sin and seek to live in peace with one another." Regardless of one's past experiences, as long as there is life, we believe that there is hope in Christ to improve one's humanity.

When we receive the bread, we know that it is symbolic of Christ's body broken for us. Jesus "took a loaf of bread ... and when he had given thanks, he broke the bread, and said, 'This is my body which is for you'" (1 Corinthians 11:24). The bread speaks to us both of Christ's suffering and His ability to sustain us. He is both the Savior who suffered for us and the one who is able to meet our every physical and spiritual need.

When you receive the bread, remember the passion of Christ, which paid for our sins. The suffering of Christ reveals the love of God for humanity. "For God so loved the world, that he gave his only Son, so that everyone who believes in him may not perish, but may have eternal life" (John 3:16). Jesus' death on the cross was the greatest expression of God's love that could ever be given.

Romans 8:32 opens our eyes to a God who did not withhold his own Son, but allowed him to die on the cross for all of us. It asks what we can imagine that God might withhold when he has already given us such a prize. And it assures us that the bread of the communion mean symbolizes God's attention to our spiritual hunger. Jesus is the Lamb of God that takes away the sins of the world.

So, when you dip the bread into the cup, remember: "In the same way Our Lord Jesus took the cup, also after supper, saying, 'This cup is the new covenant in my blood. Do this, as often as you drink it, in remembrance of me.'"

Christ's blood was poured out for the forgiveness of our sins. Because of His shed blood, we can now be fully and freely forgiven by God. Peter 1:18-19 asks us to consider how we were ransomed from the error and pointless effort we inherited from our forbears, how like cloth that can be eaten by moths are our human efforts, and how perfect is the redemption of Christ, the One with no blemish.

Christ's blood poured out is the New Covenant of grace. To be saved under the Old Covenant, we had to keep the Law perfectly. Our righteousness had to be absolutely flawless. But humanity was not able to keep the Law flawlessly.

But now, under this New Covenant of grace, our salvation does not depend upon our works. Our salvation depends upon the grace of Jesus, who died so that we might have eternal life. Jesus paid the penalty for our sins by his blood poured out on Calvary's Cross. In this New Covenant of grace, we now live for Christ by letting Christ live in us. This is what salvation is all about. We are saved and forgiven through Christ's blood.

So receive the symbols of the bread and cup with gladness and thanksgiving in your heart. We can confess our sins to God, surrender and commit ourselves fully to God's will. Because of the open invitation, we can experience fellowship, forgiveness and the blessed Hope of eternal Life.

And then Jesus concluded the supper by saying, "For as often as you eat this bread, and drink the cup, you proclaim the Lord's death until he comes." In Holy Communion we remember Christ's death and the grace in our redemption.

Questions for Reflection and Meditation

- In what ways or on what occasions am I aware of the grace given to us through Christ Jesus?

- Do I participate in Holy Communion on a regular basis?

- Talk with family members and church members about what Holy Communion means to you. Explore what Holy Communion means to them.

CHAPTER ELEVEN

Peace and the Holy Spirit

John 20:19-29

Many people attend Easter services but are not seen at church again until the next year. No pastor, from her or his vantage point in the pulpit can help but ask what it is that draws so many more on that one day than on any other Sunday of the year. Are the "Easter Christians" true believers? Or are they simply observing a social custom, perhaps placating a spouse or supposing themselves to set a good example for their children? On the other hand, could it be that somehow they are drawn to an undeniable power that somehow seems more present on that Sunday? Many faithful lay members have expressed these questions to me over the years, perhaps expressing wonder that the Holy Spirit works differently in the hearts of some than themselves.

The Good News is that every Sunday is a little Easter as we celebrate the resurrection power of God, who raised Jesus from the dead. Each Sunday great worship services are available to all. The power of the Holy Spirit is available to all. To those who knock (regularly) the door (to the Spirit) will be opened.

Prayer: Gracious God, today we give thanks for the people in our lives who ask good questions, and encourage us to grow spiritually, continue to increase our faith, and reduce our doubts as we meditate on your word. Amen.

John 20:19-29 raises questions concerning Easter Sunday, and the resurrection, which is sometimes difficult to comprehend. Many people believe in the resurrection and eternal life, and some people do not. You may have questions, and be unclear as to what you believe or what the church teaches. It is quite common for Christian people to be at different points of understanding along our spiritual journeys of faith.

The church teaches that Easter Sunday is a celebration of the Resurrection of Jesus Christ, which is understood as God's raising of Jesus Christ from death to life on the third day (Sunday) after his crucifixion (Acts 4:10; 5:30; Romans 10:9). Christ is thus alive and worshiped as the risen Lord (Philippians 2:6-11), who rules the world and is present in the world and with the church (Matthew 28:20). Easter Sunday is also a celebration of the Resurrection Life, which is understood as the new existence given to those who know the power of Jesus Christ's resurrection (Philippians 3:10), and who live in light of this reality (Westminster Dictionary of Theological Terms, Donald K. McKim, 1996.)

The Good News in our text is that it is alright to doubt and question the resurrection and to doubt and question God. I believe that struggling and asking questions about the Bible, and experiencing moments of doubt, are all part of what it means to be a people of faith who are seeking more understanding.

Henry Drummond (a Scottish scientist and evangelist who was known as a most Christ-like man, 1851-1897) once wrote about some of the differences between a doubter and an unbeliever. He wrote that a doubter is a person who searches for God and the Godly life. This is a person on a journey, a quest, a search to find God and to discover the love of God. An unbeliever isn't searching for God so much as for situations in life that bring happiness. The doubter, wrote Drummond, is a person with a "thousand questions" about life, love, purpose and more. But the unbeliever isn't questioning about God, but may be apathetic regarding God. The doubter struggles with God to live a Godly life and struggles to find the purpose of life, but this is not so with the unbeliever.

Doubts, questions and life experiences can all deepen our faith in God as experienced through Jesus Christ. There are many good questions raised in the Bible. You may recall a man named Nicodemus who came to Jesus by night. He acknowledged that Jesus was a teacher from God, and Nicodemus sought information to help his doubts. Jesus invited him to be born again of the water and the spirit. In the Book of Job, chapter 14:14, he asks, "If mortals die, will they live again? All the days of my service I would wait until my release should come." The Apostle Paul asks a great question in Romans 8:35-39, "Who will separate us from the love of Christ?" Paul concluded by saying, "I am convinced that nothing in all creation will be able to separate us from the love of God in Christ Jesus our Lord." And in John 20:25 the disciple Thomas said, "Unless I see the mark of the nails in his hands, I will not believe."

The Gospel of John tells us that on the first Easter morning there were questions, doubt and belief! It was early on the first day of the week, and while it was still dark, Mary Magdalene came to the tomb and saw the stone rolled away. She ran to tell two other disciples, and they all looked into the tomb. One disciple looked and believed. Mary remained at the tomb and saw two angels; she wondered where the body of Jesus was. After talking to the angels she turned and saw Jesus, but she believed He was the gardener. She asked a question, "Sir, if you have carried him away, tell me where you have laid him, and I will take him away." Jesus said to her, "Mary!" Mary Magdalene at first doubtful, now believed, and became the first to carry the Good News to the others. Christ Is Risen! Christ Is Risen Indeed!

On that Easter evening, John 20:19-23 says that the doors of the house where the disciples had met were locked for fear of the Jews. Jesus came and stood among them, and said "Peace be with you." Jesus then showed them his hands, feet and side, which were the marks that took his life, and verified that he was crucified and that he had died. After seeing the marks, the disciples rejoiced in the Lord. Jesus then said to them again, "Peace be with you. As the Father has sent me, so I send you." When he had said this, he breathed on them and said, "Receive the Holy Spirit. If you forgive the sins of any, they are forgiven them; if you retain the sins of any, they are retained." Jesus then sent the disciples out of their locked room and out into the world to serve as his witnesses.

Jesus visited the disciples to calm their fears, to refocus them on the mission of the church and to grant them peace and the Holy Spirit. Their mission was to go into the world and make disciples through the sharing of the good news of Jesus Christ. "The Holy Spirit" is available to each and everyone and is able to assist us in any decision-making process with wisdom and power.

Peace or Shalom is a Hebrew term used both for greeting and farewell with great richness of meaning. Peace or Shalom is a greeting stressing God's presence, and full societal and personal well-being, possible only as a gift of God. The Holy Spirit that Jesus breathes on the disciples is the third Person of the Trinity. God the Father, God the Son and God the Holy Spirit comprise the eternal Godhead. The

Holy Spirit inspired biblical writers. The Holy Spirit makes known the saving work of Jesus Christ, and the Holy Spirit is God as present in and with the church. The Holy Spirit acts to incorporate all things into the life of the triune God (Westminster Dictionary of Theological Terms, Donald K. McKim, 1996).

Philemon 4:7 tells us that the Peace which comes from God is beyond our comprehension, yet it is ours in Christ and it will guard our hearts and anxious minds when we remain in Christ.   John 14:27 says, "Peace I leave with you, my peace I give to you: I do not give to you as the world gives. Do not let your hearts be troubled and do not let them be afraid."

In John 20:24 we notice, first of all, that Thomas was absent from his small disciple group, and we do not know why. He missed a very important meeting. Because Thomas missed the meeting, and because of his historical response to missing the meeting, he is often referred to as "doubting Thomas." It is true that he doubted, but many have doubted the promises of God. Thomas is mentioned three times in the Gospel of John, and each time Thomas has something important to say.

In John chapter 11, Jesus had delayed two days in checking on his beloved friend Lazarus. Some of the disciples warned Jesus by telling Him that he must stay away from the tomb of Lazarus, where jealous and angry Jews were waiting to stone Him. They were clearly exasperated that He was determined to go to the tomb. Thomas, who was called the Twin, said to Jesus and the other disciples in verse 16, "Let us also go, that we may die with him." This was a brave statement by Thomas. This statement may also give us a clue as to why Thomas was not fearful and locked with the others behind doors._

The second time we hear from Thomas is in John 14. Jesus spoke to his disciples, calming them and telling them to still their minds and hearts. He admonished them to believe in God and also in Himself. "In my Father's house there are many dwelling places. If it were not so, I would have told you. I am going there to prepare a place for you ... and you know the way to the place where I am going." Thomas questioned Jesus in John 14:5, expressing the followers dismay, saying, in effect, "How can we know the way when we do not know what your travel plans are?" Jesus said to him, "I am the way, and the truth, and the life." Thomas did not understand what Jesus was saying and so he asked Jesus the questions. None of the other disciples expressed having difficulty with the lesson, but Thomas did. The third time we hear from Thomas is when he questions the resurrection in this text.

I do not know your spiritual history, but Jeff Hampton can be just like Thomas at times. Why does the world let people starve to death? Why is the world so mean at times? What in the world does that Bible verse mean, is that a biblical contradiction? Why do bad things happen? Why am I ill? Why do we have to lose a loved one? Why do we experience problems at work, home or at play? Why? Why? Why? Sometimes my mind just races away from me with questions.

But, in times of doubt, fear, uncertainty and unbelief, the community of faith, family and friends can be very comforting and helpful. I believe that it is important to participate in Christian fellowship and church worship because it helps us when we are doubtful.

John 20:26-29 takes place one week after the first Easter, and the disciples are again in the house. This time Thomas is present. Jesus had returned to encourage the disciples and to bless his friend Thomas. Although the doors were shut, Jesus came and stood among them and said, "Peace be with you." Then he said to Thomas, "Put your finger here and see my hands. Reach out your hand and put it in my side. Do not doubt but believe." Thomas answered him, "My Lord, and my God!" Jesus said to him, "Now Thomas, have you believed because you have seen me? Blessed are those who have not seen and yet have come to believe." Thomas is restored within the fellowship of believers. Restoration and reconciliation happen each week when people of faith come together to worship, study the Bible together and nurture one another.

Dietrich Bonhoeffer, a theologian and a German Lutheran pastor (1906-1945), in Life Together, writes these words: "It is in times of frailty and vulnerability in faith, that we most need to be in the community of faith, for when my faith is weak, I rely on the strength of my brothers and sisters in the faith; and when they are experiencing similar struggles, they come to rely upon my presence and my faith."

During a recent personal illness, I must confess that I experienced some doubtful moments, fear, uncertainty and spiritual weakness. But, each time I felt this way, the community of faith sent me a word of hope, love or encouragement that was expressed in many wonderful ways. I was thankful for their faithfulness, I relied on their strength, I grew as a Christian believer and I love them all.

Jesus responds to all of our doubts by saying, "I am the resurrection and the life. Those who believe in me, even though they die, will live, and everyone who lives and believes in me will never die" (John 11:25).

Christ Is Risen! Christ Is Risen Indeed!

Questions for Reflection and Meditation

- Have I ever felt like a "doubting Thomas?" How have I dealt with those feelings and moved on to firmer spiritual footing?

- Has a loved one or dear friend every confessed to feeling like a "doubting Thomas?" What Have I done to help her/him past that crisis of faith?

- How can my doubts lead me to a deeper faith?

- Am I willing to face my doubts?

CHAPTER TWELVE

Freedom to Say No

Luke 9:51-62

Prayer: O God, forgive us when we delay obedience to your call with excuses. Strengthen us to follow Jesus in service to the high purposes of your kingdom. We are grateful for our individual heritage and freedom and the example of the saints who have gone before us. Continue to bless this nation and world. In His name. Amen.

Jesus teaches that He must be first, or we are not following him as the greatest example in our life. Because we have the "freedom to say no," many times our choices may not coincide with the teachings of Christ.

When we are fully invested in the Christian experience, we find ourselves constantly responding: to the indwelling Holy Spirit that nudges our conscience, to the example of Jesus, and to the Word of God. What do I mean by the phrase, "fully invested in the Christian experience? I mean being able to look yourself in the mirror each morning and see more than flesh, blood, and a bad hair day. I mean being able to look into that mirror and say to yourself about that image looking back at you, "a child of God." I'm not talking about prideful self-righteousness, of course. I mean the satisfying feeling that comes to a believer when she/he sees in that morning mirror a real person who, in spite of real struggles of faith, has taken steps—positive steps whether small or large—on a daily walk with Christ.

We have the freedom to say "yes" to the silent call of the Spirit or not-so-silent requests from the church. Sometimes our responses are yes, sometimes no, and sometimes we respond with maybe, or in a few minutes, or in a few years. Because we have the freedom to say no, we often place conditions on our responses to God's call. Since July 4, 1776, the United States of America continues the construction of a free society, where people have the "freedom to say no" or yes, to formal or informal religious experiences. Independence Day is the founding and anniversary of the day on which the Declaration of Independence was adopted by the Continental Congress.

Within a free society, the call to discipleship can be avoided with a variety of excuses. Human freedom is the condition in which humans may freely choose their own behavior and situations, without external force or oppression. Societal freedom enables human freedom to operate. Christian freedom is the freedom of the Christian, on the basis of the work of Jesus Christ by the Holy Spirit, to be free from the power of sin in all its forms. John 8:36 says, "So if the Son makes you free, you will be free indeed" (Westminster Dictionary of Theological Terms, Donald K. McKim).

In Luke 9, there are about six months remaining before Jesus' death and resurrection, and he is teaching five of his followers – James and John, two of the 12 disciples, and three other followers who were probably not of the 12. All five of these men found themselves responding contrary to Jesus' will.

Through this story we can discover what discipleship means to us today. Jesus was determined to go to Jerusalem; in fact "he set his face to go to Jerusalem." Jesus is faced with problems from his disciples and from others who are reluctant to follow. So Jesus uses these moments to teach us what it means to follow him as the number one priority in our lives. By studying the journey of Jesus, we always learn something about our personal journeys.

Jesus and his disciples were on their way from Galilee to Jerusalem, and Samaria lies between the two places. Jesus, knowing the long history of Jews and Samaritans, wanted to travel through the village of Samaria. He sent messengers ahead of him to make preparations, but they did not receive him. When his disciples James and John saw it, they said something like this, "Lord, shall we call upon a Heavenly fire bolt to strike those slackers and burn them to a crisp?" That wasn't what Jesus had in mind. Turning to his disciples with an arched eyebrow (can't you just see it?), he rebuked them. Jesus admonished them; he reprimanded them; he chewed them out; he reproached them. Jesus conducted some up-close-and-personal teaching with his disciples, and then they went on to another village (vv. 51-56).

The disciples wanted revenge when Jesus was rejected. They wanted to destroy the Samaritans with fire from heaven like Elijah did in 2 Kings 1:10-12. We remember that Elijah called down fire from heaven to demonstrate the true power of God, because the king of Samaria had turned to other gods. But James and John were not acting in the same spirit as Elijah. James and John were being vengeful by wanting to punish the Samaritans. But Jesus did not come to destroy. He came to save. James and John were wrong and maybe prejudiced. Elijah called down fire from heaven to show people the true power of God, not for vengeance. And Jesus rebuked James and John so that they might examine themselves and believe in him.

Ezra 4:1-3 tells us that when the Jews returned from the Babylonian captivity and began to rebuild the temple in Jerusalem, the Samaritans wanted to help the Jews. But because the Samaritans were a mixture of pagans and Jews, the Jews refused the Samaritans' help. Then the Samaritans separated themselves and built their own temple. Therefore, the Jews and the Samaritans had no dealings with each other. The Gospel of John 4:9 tells us that a Samaritan woman said to Jesus, "How dare you, a Jew, ask a drink of me, a woman of Samaria?'Jews and Samaritans do not share drinking cups." This is one of the historical reasons for the refusal of the Samaritans in Luke 9:52.

As Jesus and the disciples continue on the road to Jerusalem, Jesus talks with three potential followers. The first person made a promise that he could not keep by saying, "I will follow you wherever you go." The second person did not want to follow Jesus until he had buried his father, and the third person promised to follow Jesus after saying farewell to the people he loved. Jesus does not reject these three persons, but he does tell them that they are not ready for the kingdom of God.

When the first person said to Jesus, "I will follow you wherever you go," Jesus said to him, "Foxes have holes, and birds of the air have nests; but the Son of Man has nowhere to lay his head (vv. 57-58). To this very day, it is common for missionaries, ministers and many other vocations around the world not to own a permanent residence. Jesus was saying to this would-be follower that he had never owned a permanent home, and that it was possible for followers of him to suffer from the lack of food, clothing and shelter. Jesus was preparing them for the uncertain days that were quickly approaching. If the disciples were going to carry the gospel to the utter most parts of the world, they would have to walk by faith and not by sight.

At any given time, more than 50 million people are homeless somewhere in the world, and some are fleeing for their lives. Christian people pray for and reach out to the homeless of the world, providing comfort and shelter.

Christian people also reach out and pray for the millions of people who are without a permanent church home as well. All people need a place to grow and develop their faith – somewhere among a body of believers who nurture one another in the faith. Everyone needs a Christian home, and a church home – a place to feel loved, welcome, wanted and needed. Jesus is not saying that he never slept in a bed or house, but as he approached Jerusalem, he was saying that the world had not realized who he was and that he had been rejected.

To another he said, "Follow me." But he said, "Lord, first let me go and bury my father." But Jesus said to him, "Let the dead bury their own dead; but as for you, go and proclaim the kingdom of God (vv. 59-60). This second man makes an excuse that produces an answer that sounds disrespectful coming from Jesus. But Jesus was not saying to this man to forget his love for his father and not to make any final arrangements. Jesus is saying that when Christians bury Christians, the preaching of the gospel is the most important thing. None of our many different kinds of losses are more important than staying centered in Christ, the hope of the world. Jesus is telling him not to focus on death, but to focus on the kingdom, because death is not the end of the story. So Jesus says go and proclaim the kingdom of God.

A third person said, "I will follow you, Lord; but let me first say farewell to those at my home." Jesus said to him, "No one who puts a hand to the plow and looks back is fit for the kingdom of God" (vv. 61-62).

Sometimes when we look back and hope for the past, it is not what we really need. In Exodus 16:3, the children of Israel looked back. "If only we had died by the hand of the Lord, in the land of Egypt, when we sat by the fleshpots and ate our fill of bread; for you have brought us out into this wilderness to kill this whole assembly with hunger." Genesis 19:26 tells us that, "But Lot's wife, behind him, looked back, and she became a pillar of salt." Christian people look straight ahead, "But strive first for the kingdom of God and his righteousness, and all these things will be given to you as well" (Matthew 6:33). The gospel causes us to look straight ahead and not backwards. We should not want to lose the progress that has been made in medicine, or the progress that has been made in race relations. We do not want to lose the progress that has been made in international affairs, or the progress that has been made in our spiritual development, along with the development of our family and Christian relationships. With both hands on the plow, Christian people are looking forward to peace and reconciliation with all humanity.

When listening to the call of God in our lives, the vision of the kingdom is our focus. And when we experience rejection, we seek God who never rejects us. Sometimes, like James and John, we lose sight of the kingdom, and we want fire to rain down on people who reject us, or look different – people who do not believe as we do, or people who may be less or more fortunate. The common response to rejection is to reject more. But Jesus tells James and John to respond with grace. Jesus would not have any part of the disciples' rejection of the Samaritans because of centuries of hard feelings. The focus in our text is not on how the Samaritans responded to Jesus. The focus is on how Jesus responded to the Samaritans who had the "freedom to say no."

The disciples wanted the Samaritans consumed by fire, but Jesus reached out to the Samaritans. The Gospel of Luke tells the Parable of the Good Samaritan, "But a Samaritan while traveling came near him; and when he saw him, he was moved with pity ... Which of these was a neighbor to the man who fell into the hands of the robbers? ... The one who showed him mercy" – the Samaritan (Luke 10:33, 36-37). The Gospel of Luke also tells us about the healing of 10 lepers, "Then one of them, when he saw that he was healed, turned back, praising God with a loud voice. He laid on the ground at Jesus' feet and thanked him. And he was a Samaritan. Then Jesus said to him, 'Get up and go on your way; your faith has made you well'" (Luke 17:15-16, 19).

The Acts of the Apostles records that at the Ascension of Jesus, he gives his disciples some final instructions. "But you will receive power when the Holy Spirit has come upon you; and you will be my witnesses in Jerusalem, in all Judea, and Samaria and to the ends of the earth" (Acts 1:8). In Acts 8:14, 17 we read, "Now when the apostles at Jerusalem heard that Samaria had accepted the word of God, they sent Peter and John to them ... Then Peter and John laid their hands on them, and they received the Holy Spirit."

"Foxes have holes, and birds of the air have nests; but the Son of Man has nowhere to lay his head" (Luke 9:58). Jesus understands when we feel rejected, lonely, or are without a home or church home. "Let the dead bury their own dead; but as for you, go and proclaim the kingdom of God" (Luke 9:60). Say a prayer, and let go of the things that are of the past and are gone – things that we mortals have no control of. Proclaim the Kingdom, because our losses are not the end of the story. "No one who puts a hand to the plow and looks back is fit for the kingdom of God" (Luke 9:62). We have come too far to turn around now, and God has not brought us this far to abandon us. With both hands on the plow, Christians press forward.

Although we have the "freedom to say no," to reject or

receive at will, God never gives up on us. The Spirit of Jesus is available to meet each of us, at our different points of need, right now and always!

Questions for Reflection and Meditation

• Am I okay with my personal record of listening to and obeying the Spirit of God within me when a response to the call of Christ is required?

• Do I sometimes try to avoid being called to particular responsibilities in the church? Have I talked through my reaction to those invitations with family or friends in the church?

• Am I comfortable saying "no" or "yes" to requests made in God's name?

• Do I harbor grudges about others' a) failure to respond to what seem to me to be clear calls from the Spirit or the Church, or b) seemingly excessive investment of time in Church work?

CHAPTER THIRTEEN

Sin and Forgiveness

Psalm 51:1-17

Prayer: Almighty God, your love for us is truly amazing, and you forgive the sins of all who are penitent: Create and make in us new hearts, that we may obtain remission and forgiveness through Jesus Christ our Lord. Amen.

Lent is the season of preparation before the celebration of Easter, running forty days, not counting Sundays. Lent begins on Ash Wednesday and ends on Holy Saturday. Historically, people marked times of fasting, prayer and repentance by placing ashes on their foreheads, as in the Book of Job, chapter 42:6, "therefore I despise myself, and repent in dust and ashes." So, on Ash Wednesday, we gather in observance of a season of holy Lent. For Christian people the 40 days consist of sober reflection, self-examination, repentance and spiritual redirection. We recognize our shortcomings or areas in our life that we can improve upon, and then resolve to change our behavior through prayer, fasting, self-denial and through the reading and meditation on God's Word.

We are invited to reflect upon and write down a particular area in our life that we would like to improve – or write down a sin, a new commitment or sacrifice.

Through worship and the imposition of ashes, we participate in the call to repentance and reconciliation. By having ashes imposed on our foreheads, we remember that God created us out of the dust of the earth. The ashes are a sign of our mortality, a sign to us of God's gracious gift of everlasting life. The dab of ashes on our foreheads remind us to repent and believe the gospel.

Psalm 51 is a beautiful prayer for cleansing and pardon. The psalmist developed guilt, and acknowledged it to God by confessing: "Have mercy on me, O God, according to your steadfast love; according to your abundant mercy blot out my transgressions." What sets this psalm apart from many others is that the psalmist's complaint involves personal sinfulness. Verse two says, "Wash me thoroughly from my iniquity, and cleanse me from my sin." Sin and forgiveness is what this psalm is about. It is also about human nature and God's nature. This psalm is about how we behave even at our best as individuals, families and churches. Our human condition is a sinful condition. But the good news is that God is willing to forgive sinners and is able to re-create people. The psalmist prays and asks God for forgiveness. God answers this prayer and forgives the sins of the psalmist. Sin is a powerful and persistent reality, but God's grace is a more powerful and enduring reality.

No matter what we have done in the past, no matter how many times we have done it, no matter how badly we may have strayed, we too can experience God's forgiveness. Each one of us, whether we realize it or not, has a need to be forgiven. Romans 3:23-24 plainly says that every person fails to measure up to God's expectations, that each of us fails to fulfill Christ's idea for His people, that the only way we reach justification is through the free gift of grace, and that the only path to that free gift is through Christ. Psalm 51 is a model of how we can receive God's forgiveness in our lives.

There are four aspects of repentance that are outlined in this Psalm. The first aspect of repentance is recognition that sin has obtained control over one's life. "For I know my transgressions and my sin is ever before me." Here the psalmist admits to sin. We can not pretend we can hide our sins from God. God knows when we do, or say, or think something wrong. But God wants us to admit it.

The second aspect of repentance is to understand that sin is directed, not only against ourselves, or others, but primarily against God. The first portion of verse four says: "Against you, you alone, have I sinned, and done what is evil in your sight." The psalmist realizes that sin has taken place against God. No matter how badly we harm someone else, the most terrible part of sin is that it violates God's holiness. This may be hard to accept. Sin and its consequences are pervasive, and it is a failure to honor God.

The third aspect of repentance is to be willing to assume full responsibility for one's behavior. The last portion of verse four assures us that we are cleansed of our sinful "his judgment record," that God now sees us as blameless, that we have nothing to fear of. Our Lord does not want us to fill our days with fearful expectations of his wrath. God wants us to find joy in His redemption. The first letter of John 1:9, the writer says something like this: Once we confess our sins, the Lord keeps his part of the bargain in a spirit of loving justice. That includes complete forgiveness for our transgressions. He welcomes us and forgets our previous wrongdoings. Genuine confession of sin happens when we are willing to accept full responsibility for our actions, and then experience God's amazing forgiveness.

The fourth aspect of repentance is to abandon all claims of worthiness or entitlement. "Indeed, I was born guilty, a sinner when my mother conceived me." The psalmist is simply confessing that the problem is not just what has happened, but with humanity as a whole. We need to recognize that we are sinners by nature. While sin is a matter of individual decision, it also has a corporate dimension that affects us, despite our best intentions and decisions. The psalmist receives forgiveness and blessing from God, and the broken relationship is healed. These steps help us to realize that God's mercy and steadfast love create the possibility of forgiveness. Psalm 51 is a good model of what true confession involves. The psalmist responds, imploring God to use his mouth to praise God. After confession of sin, we must believe by faith Jesus' promise to forgive us. When we receive forgiveness and experience reconciliation, we are filled with gratitude and praise for God. Reconciliation happens as a result of God's willingness to forgive and the result is a new creation. The reconciled are then entrusted with the message of reconciliation. God's forgiveness is a wonderful gift, and when we receive it we are compelled to share with others. When we share, we participate in the ministry of Christ, the ministry of reconciliation.

Throughout history people have been forgiven, justified and reconciled to God. By the grace of God, a persistently disobedient people become partners with God in "an everlasting covenant" (Isaiah 55:3). By the grace of God, confused and disobedient disciples of Jesus become known as those "who have been turning the world upside down." By the grace of God, Saul, the former murderer, becomes Paul, ambassador for Christ. And by the Grace of God, all of us have come this far by faith, trusting in the Lord. God's Grace is truly amazing and available for all.

What does the Apostle Paul say in II Corinthians 5:17-20? First, he writes that once a person affirms belief in Christ that believer is a new creation. The old person is gone and a new one stands in her/his place. The transformation is a gift from a God who makes his peace with the believer through no effort or intention of the person but through Christ. This is God's gift of a ministry of reconciliation. It is God's reaching out to us, so that we may reach out (reconcile) with others in this world and to God. It brings God's assurance that he no longer will hold our failings against us. And it includes our commission as ministers for Christ. God sends individual believers to take his Word to the world, and we can only fulfill that commission if we are reconciled both to God and to our fellow humans.

Finally, the transformed psalmist was a living sacrifice. "The sacrifice acceptable to God is a broken and contrite heart, O God, you will not despise" (v. 17). The psalmist was able to discern the will of God and participate with God in transforming the world. By the grace of God, amid the persistent reality of human sinfulness, there is a new creation.

Paul says, "I appeal to you therefore, brothers and sisters, by the mercies of God, to present your bodies as a living sacrifice, holy and acceptable to God, which is your spiritual worship. Do not be conformed to this world, but be transformed by the renewing of your minds, so that you may discern what is the will of God – what is good and acceptable and perfect."

If you are carrying around a burden of guilt, Lent is the perfect time to share your burdens with God. Maybe you just need to experience God's forgiveness in a new way and be reconciled. Why not simply confess your sins, and praise God for God's forgiveness. Psalm 51 teaches us that it is by God's Grace that we are forgiven. And we need forgiveness so that our relationship with God can be restored.

"Create in me a clean heart, O God, and put a new and right spirit within me. Do not cast me away from your presence, and do not take your Holy Spirit from me. Restore to me the joy of your salvation, and sustain in me a willing spirit. Then I will teach transgressors your ways, and sinners will return to you" (vv. 10-13).

Questions for Reflection and Meditation

• Am I courageous enough to truly repent and be a new creation? What does it mean to me to allow God to make me an entirely new creation?

• How many times have I actually been present at a Maundy Thursday service...and what special meaning did I find in it?

• Am I able to share my burdens with God?

• Do I open my heart for cleansing through the Holy Spirit, or are there ways in which I hold back?

CHAPTER FOURTEEN

Receive

Luke 1:26-38

Prayer: Grant us to believe in the Baby Jesus Christ, our Lord and our Savior, that our faith may never be found wanting in your sight. Help us to serve you with all our being. Help others to receive the gift of the Christ child and serve through him, who lives and reigns with you, and the Holy Spirit, one God, now and forever. Amen.

I expect everyone reading this expects to receive a gift on Christmas Day. Most people I know give a great deal of thought to the gifts they expect to give and receive on Christmas Day. How about your own list: how many people are on your list? Are you one of those people who have more than one list for Christmas giving? What about the lists that include you—the lists of people who plan to give you a gift on Christmas? Some people, for various reasons, may not expect to receive a gift this Christmas. Some people, because of death, divorce, or other change in circumstance, may not expect to be on anyone's list. Some have great expectations for giving and receiving; others expect to receive very little— even nothing.

Which feels better to you – to receive a gift or to give a gift? Every Christmas, Christian people continue the rich tradition of receiving and sharing the gift of the Baby Jesus. I am not sure which one I have enjoyed the most – receiving Christ as my personal Savior or sharing Christ with others.

The Good News of Christmas is that everyone, the whole world, receives a gift. Everyone is on the list. Our task is to receive the gift that has been given with open hearts year after year and to share the gift of the Christ Child, our Savior, with as many people as we can. The Virgin Mary, the mother of Jesus, sets a wonderful example of how we are to receive this gift from God to all creation. The greatest sign that you have received the gift of Jesus is expressed in sharing with others. Are you ready to receive the miracle of Christmas for the first time or for the 100th time? We do not give to one another only once, but we continue to give year after year. And God continues to give to us.

Thirty years after the death of Jesus, Luke wrote about the miracle of His birth and its meaning in the lives of His followers. How do you prepare your heart to receive the miracle of Christmas? We spend a great deal of time, energy, and money preparing our homes for the outward signs of the Christmas season. How do you prepare your mind, your spirit, to receive Christ again? When we accept the Christ Child, we accept our faith. We respond by sharing Christ with others, giving and making disciples. During Advent we prepare to receive Christ all over again, and some people will receive Christ for the first time. People will overcome their doubts and fears, and trust God – the Hope of the Christ Child.

At the close of an advent season, you may know of someone who has never received the gift of the Christ Child. Someone who is living without the true gift of Christmas. This person may be a family member, friend, co-worker or someone we may not know. We share in the Spirit of Christ because we know that the Spirit is highly contagious. Our prayer should be that every person will receive the gifts of the Spirit and then produce the fruits of the Spirit, which are love, joy, peace, kindness, etc. Every person needs to develop the faith to receive Christ in their heart. Receive first, then nurture and develop your faith. Mary first receives the gift, and then nurtures the Baby Jesus to adulthood.

Are you ready to receive gifts that are too small, too large, the wrong color? The Gospel of Luke gives details of the unique (Nativity) origin of Jesus, and he tells us how Jesus' birth was foretold. The first chapter of Luke tells us about the births of John the Baptist and Jesus. We are told about the pregnancy of Elizabeth, which was amazing because of her age. The pregnancy of Mary was even more amazing. Mary was unmarried and a virgin, but engaged to Joseph. Mary was very young (13 to 17 years old). God, through the angel Gabriel, told Mary she was soon to become the mother of the Son of God. Jesus would be fully human and fully God. Mary, knowing that she was a virgin, asked how this could happen. Gabriel told her that God himself would cause her to become pregnant. The Christmas story gives us confidence to receive the gift of Jesus with excitement and joy as Mary did. Jesus would be the Messiah, the heir of David's ancient throne, both divine and human, God's Son. This is the story of Mary's fear, wonder and submission.

Mary lived in the village of Nazareth, in the hilly area southwest of the Sea of Galilee. Her fiancée, or husband-to-be, was Joseph, who was a descendent of Israel's greatest king, David. Mary's ancestry was more complex. We know that Mary's relative Elizabeth was a descendent of the original high priest, Aaron, of the tribe of Levi (Luke 1:5). But Mary also may be a descendent herself of David of the tribe of Judah on her father's side, and Luke's genealogy (3:23-38) may actually trace Mary's lineage, though this is disputed.

Hebrew prophets foretold what we call the first Coming of Jesus the Messiah. These prophets foretold his human ancestry, his birthplace, where he would grow up, details of his public ministry, when he would come, how he would be rejected and how he would die and be resurrected. The Savior would have to be human, sinless and God.

Without Christ there would be no Christmas. Before Christ there was no Christmas. The world now pauses to remember the birth of a more than average Baby Boy, our Savior. The entire history of the world centers on the birth of Christ – the Promised Messiah, the Prince of Peace, the Hope in Jesus. This birth was promised, planned and pure.

A normal birth happens between two people, but this was not a normal birth. Never was there one like it before, nor will there be one later. Prophets told about the birth of Jesus 700 years in advance. God told the Jewish people that their Savior would be born from a virgin and that he would be both man and God. This is only one of 100 specific predictions in the Bible that describe the coming of Jesus.

The prophet Isaiah told the story 700 years before Jesus was born, thus the miracle of Jesus' birth was a fulfillment of Old Testament prophecy. More than 730 years earlier, God predicted that a "sign" of the Messiah to the Jews would be a virgin-born Son (Isa. 7:14) and that this child would be both human and divine (Isa. 9:6). This is what Gabriel is reminding Mary of in verses 32 and 33. The birth of Jesus was not only promised to us, but it was a well-planned birth. Adam and Eve received the first promise of the coming Christ, the Messiah. The Prophet Micah told us the town where Christ would be born. In Micah, chapter 5, verse 2, the Old Testament audience became the first to know that the Messiah would be born into one of the "little clans of Judah," to the people of Bethlehem. How remarkable is that? Seven hundred years before His birth, Jesus' birthplace and clan were predicted.

Not only was the birth of Jesus promised, planned, and announced, but it was a uniquely pure birth. Read about it in Matthew, Chapter 1, verses 18 through 23. What do we learn there? We read that Christ was born of a virgin, a young woman who had not been visited by her chosen man. This was a miracle birth, a supernatural birth. From the day Jesus was born, he was born to do God's will. Jesus had one mission and one purpose on earth, and that was to do God's will. Jesus willingly accepted the burden placed on him. We, too, only have one mission and one purpose. God has a plan for each child that is born.

"Therefore the Lord himself will give you a sign. Look, the young woman is with child and shall bear a son, and shall name him Immanuel" (Isaiah 7:14).

"For a child has been born for us, a son given to us; authority rests upon his shoulders; and he is named Wonderful Counselor, Mighty God, Everlasting Father, Prince of Peace" (Isaiah 9:6).

Mary received assurance that God will provide the miracle of birth in her just as he made her relative Elizabeth pregnant when she thought it impossible. Mary was told to stop fretting. Many Christians have problems with the Virgin Birth. This is OK if you are at this point. Verse 32 also tells us that Jesus is both human and divine – fully God and fully human. Jesus is the second person of the Trinity, the incarnation of God.

When Elizabeth was six months pregnant, the angel Gabriel appeared to Mary, a virgin engaged to a man named Joseph, of the house of David. The virgin was surprised by Gabriel's presence, but the angel reassured her, telling her that she was favored in the sight of God (Luke 1:26-28).

Receive the Gift, and the divine presence of God through our faith is now conceivable among us humans. Nothing will be impossible. Think of that when you bring the salutation to another, as one of God's own divine messengers, "The

Lord be with you." And wait with joyful anticipation for the response, "And also with you." There is much favor – heavenly, holy, blessed favor – to spread about. The Lord is with you. We can receive the God who is coming and is with us. When God visits, would God have good news or bad news for you? But what if God is coming with good news, not to put us down for our sins but to save us from our sins with the gift of the Christ Child?

"Mary was greatly troubled, full of fear, but the Angel said, 'Do not be afraid, Mary, you have found favor with God.'" Mary could have resisted God, but she responded by receiving the gift of the Christ Child (vv. 29-30).

"And now, you will conceive in you womb and bear a son, and you will name him Jesus" (v. 31).

The virgin birth and the fact that Jesus was both fully man and God were necessary in order for Jesus to be our Savior. The punishment for sin is death. God provided an innocent substitute to pay for our sins. A sinless human was needed, and he would also have to be God. His mother, Mary, was human, and his Father was God. Jesus' conception was very unusual; in fact, it was a miracle. This was not some myth or legend. This event was foretold hundreds of years in advance. Jesus' birth was also necessary in order for Jesus to be our substitute and receive the punishment we deserve so that we can receive eternal life with God.

Verse 32 tells us that the Messiah—Jesus—would have many glorious titles. He would be called "the Son of the Most High," and reign upon the throne of his forebear, David. Elsewhere we read of other titles: "Prince of Peace," "Mighty Counselor," et cetera. What would the future hold for Mary's Child?

Mary was told that her child would grow to be a man who would reign over the house of Jacob in perpetuity. How could she even imagine giving birth to a son who would be a King...let alone a king who would reign beyond any conception of a life expectancy?

In verse 34 we read that Mary—probably overcome with anxiety and doubt—retorted, asking how she—a virgin— could possibly conceive any child (let alone the child of God. Imagine how alarmed Mary must have been at the angelic announcement. Surely the prediction that she would have a child when she was not yet recognized by her family and community as fully married must have sounded—on some level—as an accusation. Mary knew herself to be a good young woman. She knew that there was no biological explanation for her to be pregnant. She responded with wonder and faith at the announcement of this miracle birth. It is OK to question God. Mary asked, "How?" Questions cause us to grow and learn. Mary had a faith question, not doubt.

"The angel said to her, 'The Holy Spirit will come upon you, and the power of the Most High will overshadow you; therefore the child to be born will be holy; he will be called Son of God" (v. 35). How would Jesus be conceived?

The answer was a referral to the remarkable pregnancy of Mary's aged relative Elizabeth, who conceived and was then six months pregnant, despite being said to be barren. The message for Mary: God is capable of doing in your body and in your life what has also been done in Elizabeth's body and life. God can do anything. God can cause a virgin to conceive, an old woman to have a child and the promised descendant of David to be born. The promise of a long, peaceful reign is God's to fulfill.

"Then Mary said, 'Here am I, the servant of the Lord; let it be with me according to your word.' Then the angel departed from her" (v. 38).

Mary's response to the Angel's announcement has been a source of joy and strength to millions who have received the Christ Child as their personal Savior. "Here am I, the servant of the Lord." Even before Jesus was conceived, Mary obeyed and made room for Jesus in her life. She did not know what the future would hold for her, but she was willing. We are willing servants. We are submissive to God. Mary offered herself to God. Are you willing to give yourself to God? Mary was dependent on God to bring his will to pass in her life, not by her own power. For all things are possible with God. God does not want us to earn our way to heaven. God wants us to trust Jesus; this is all that it takes to enter into a relationship with Christ. But we cannot earn salvation, do it ourselves or do it on our own.

Mary received the Savior of the world with gratitude, despite her fears of what others might think. She quickly overcame her doubts and concerns and offered herself as a "servant of the Lord." For nothing is impossible with God. Mary accepts the direction for her life, given by God.

The Angel Gabriel said to Mary, "Greetings favored one! The Lord is with you." And so I say to you: the Lord be with you always!

Questions for Reflection and Meditation

- Prophets foretold the clan into which Jesus would be born hundreds of years before He came. What does it mean to you that Jesus was born into an obscure clan, in a town where peoples' expectations were limited?

- Do I believe in miracles?

- Am I willing to give myself to God—even if I cannot logically understand what is being asked of me?

- When did I last respond like Mary, "Here am I...?" Can I explain now how it felt to be that receptive to the Holy Spirit?

CHAPTER FIFTEEN

Called Into Discipleship

John 1:43-51

Prayer: Almighty God, you have given each of us unique gifts and called us into discipleship to serve others. Help us listen to your call so that we may know our gifts and reach out to meet the needs of your world, through Jesus Christ our Lord. Amen.

In the United Methodist Church, Human Relations Day is usually the Sunday before the observance of Dr. Martin Luther King Jr.'s birthday. Human Relations Day calls the Church to recognize the right of all God's children in realizing their potential as human beings in relationship with each other.

God calls people to a right relationship with humanity, and into discipleship – through the Spirit and through other people. A disciple is a follower of Jesus Christ who accepts and assists in spreading the gospel in many ways. The following five questions are for reflection only. (1) Have you ever felt God calling you into discipleship? (2) If God is calling you into discipleship, what is God calling you to do to enhance better human relations or to extend hospitality?

In the key text for this study, Philip and Nathanael are prime examples of persons who were called into discipleship. And on Human Relations Day, Dr. King is a prime example of a person in more modern times who was called into discipleship. When we listen through prayer, we can feel and hear God leading us to a meaningful relationship with humanity. To help us practice our calling, God gives us certain spiritual gifts. Every believer receives at least one gift, and some people may receive several.

(3) If you have been called into discipleship, what is your spiritual gift(s), and how are you using your gift(s) to serve others? In Paul's first letter to the Corinthians, chapter 12:7 says "to each is given the manifestation of the Spirit for the common good." The first letter of Peter, chapter 4:10 says, "Like good stewards of the manifold grace of God, serve one another with whatever gift each of you has received." Spiritual gifts are given "for the common good" to "serve one another."

Philip had at least two spiritual gifts: apostle and evangelist. Nathanael, who was also known as Bartholomew, appears to have the gifts of discernment and evangelism. Dr. King certainly had the spiritual gifts of proclamation, servant hood, encouragement and visionary leadership.

Within the Gospel of John, we witness God calling people into discipleship through Jesus and through others. On Human Relations Day, we are reminded to look for the good in others, to use our spiritual gifts and to call people into discipleship.

"The next day Jesus decided to go to Galilee. He found Philip and said to him, 'Follow me'" (v. 43).

Philip was from a large city, Bethsaida, where Jews and Gentiles often worked together, which was a good example of the gospel in action. Nathanael was from Cana where Jesus would later perform his first two miracles – the wedding at Cana (John 2:1-11) and the healing of an official's son (John 4:46-54). Jesus decides to go to Galilee; he sees the good in Philip and says, "Follow me." Philip then goes and finds Nathanael to share the good news. Philip describes Jesus to Nathanael as the fulfillment of the Old Testament.

His response to Philip was, "Can anything good come out of Nazareth?" He is first doubtful and not very impressed with Nazareth, but later discerns the truth. Philip responded to his skepticism by saying, "Come and see." He is sure that Nathanael will be blessed by meeting Jesus. When we invite or call people into discipleship, and they respond with skepticism, saying "come and see" or "please visit any church" is much better than a theological debate. Consider how surprised Nathanial was when Jesus approached him. Scripture tells us that Jesus knew—even before speaking to him—that Nathanael was a man in whom no fault could be found. Nathanael asked how Jesus knew his reputation. Jesus replied that He saw Nathaniel in a specific setting ("under a Fig tree") even before Philip approached him (vv. 47-48).

Jesus appears to reference Psalm 32:2, "Happy are those to whom the Lord imputes no iniquity, and in whose spirit there is no deceit." Jesus shows a sense of humor because "Israel" was the new name given to Jacob (Gen 32:28) who had been deceitful (Gen 27:34-36) with his father Isaac. The name Jacob meant deceitful or conniving. So Jesus is saying that Nathanael is truly a descendent of Israel and not of the deceiver Jacob. Jesus also displays prophetic insight with his knowledge about Nathanael "under the fig tree," which was an Old Testament symbol of safety for the Israelites (I Kings 4:25).

Nathanael responds by affirming that Jesus, whom he identifies as a teacher, is surely "Son of God! You are the King of Israel!'" (v. 49).

Perhaps we can learn from the way Nathaniel was brought into faith. He was called into discipleship by Philip's personal witness and by Jesus' affirmation of his gifts, which caused his original skepticism to be transformed into belief. Jesus promised Nathanael that he would see the angels of God ascending and descending on a ladder set up on the earth, with the top of it reaching to heaven. Jesus is that ladder that connects heaven and earth providing access to God (Gen. 28:12). Nathanael and Philip became great witnesses for Christ.

(4) If you have not felt God calling you into discipleship, are you seeking to know God's purpose and direction for you life, your relationships, your family and your vocation? God empowers humanity to minister in ways that use our spiritual gifts to serve one another. I have personally felt God calling me into discipleship. It felt like a strong, uncontrollable desire to serve others. Individuals encouraging me also affirmed my heart-felt desire to proclaim the gospel of Christ and to administer the sacraments of Communion and Baptism. But the process of answering God's call was troublesome at times and joyful at others until I finally responded by faith and put my total trust in God.

However, the call to ordained ministry is very small when compared to the masses that have been called into discipleship. You may have answered the call by driving the church van, serving in one of the many groups in the church, reading to children, visiting others, calling others, giving financial gifts or sharing your faith. You may answer the call into discipleship through whatever career you have chosen by putting God first, and serving others. There are people all around you who would love to share with you their personal ministry.

The Good News is that every person is capable of experiencing a sense of calling into discipleship. The call to be a disciple of Jesus Christ is a sense of realizing that "this is what I must do, this is who I am and this is where

I need to serve." Individuals who have answered the call into discipleship feel a deep sense of fulfillment, peace, happiness, love and joy. We are given spiritual gifts to help us share with others in the community for building up the body of Christ in practical ways.

(5) Do you want to know your spiritual gift(s)? There are four locations in three books of the Bible that refer to more than 20 spiritual gifts. These foundational gifts can be applied in many forms to your present vocation to help you serve humanity. Some gifts are named in all four lists, while others appear in only one list. I will name each gift only once. Look at the more than 20 spiritual gifts and see if you recognize one that you may have – or you may have several.

The letter of Paul to the Romans, chapter 12:6-8, lists the spiritual gifts of proclamation, servanthood, teaching the faith, encouragement, generosity, nurturing, leadership and mercy. Paul, in his first letter to the Corinthians, chapter 12:8-10, adds wisdom, knowing, faith, healing, miracles, discernment, tongues and interpretation of tongues. In that same letter, chapter 12:28-30, Paul adds apostleship, helping, visionary and managing leadership. Lastly, in his letter to the Ephesians, chapter 4:11, Paul adds evangelism and shepherding.

The Bible also mentions many other characteristics of Christians that can be directly applied to the more than 20 foundational gifts. Some examples are intercession, missionary, writing, celibacy, voluntary poverty, martyrdom, artistry, craftsmanship, vocal and instrumental music and hospitality. If you did not hear your gift named specifically, then try applying your gift through one of the foundational gifts. Example, you may have the gift of proclamation through music, dance or administration duties.

Philip, Nathanael and Dr. Martin Luther King Jr.

responded to God's call and to the needs of their time by using their spiritual gifts. On Human Relations Day we are reminded that God calls humanity into discipleship and that we are given gifts to serve one another for the common good. When we observe the birthday of Dr. King, we remember his vision for all people to serve and love one another.

Dr. King, in his sermon titled "The Drum Major Instinct," said, "... Everybody can be great, because everybody can serve. You don't have to have a college degree to serve. You don't have to make your subject and your verb agree to serve. You don't have to know about Plato and Aristotle to serve ... You only need a heart full of grace, a soul generated by love. And you can be that servant." Dr. King concluded this sermon by quoting a song about helping others as we journey through life.

The Gospel of John was written for a purpose. Chapter 20:31 says, "But these are written so that you may come to believe that Jesus is the Messiah, the Son of God, and that through believing you may have life in his name." Without a vision of God's will for us we are lost. God is calling people to be servants to one another for the common good. And we all need one another to help us hear God's directions. God is calling; do you hear the call into discipleship?

Questions for Reflection and Meditation

• Can anything good come out of _____ [my hometown]? In what way would I be an example of something good from my hometown?

• Do I know what my spiritual gifts are?

• Have I shared and developed them?

- Do I, like Dr. King, have a favorite hymn or song that expresses my faith? How do I feel when I sing that song in Worship? Do I ever sing it in private?

CHAPTER SIXTEEN

The Transfiguration of our Lord

Luke 9:28-36

Prayer: God of truth, you lead us to the mountaintop in prayer to see the glory of your Son revealed. Grant that when we come away, our faces are changed, our purpose is renewed and our ministries are confirmed. We pray in Jesus' name, through whose power we are being transformed daily to life in your glorious image. Amen.

Transfiguration Sunday is the last Sunday before Lent, marking Christ's transfiguration on the mountain with Elijah and Moses. Lent is the period of penitence and fasting observed 40 weekdays starting Ash Wednesday and lasting until Easter.

Transition means to change from one form, stage or style to another, and to transform is to change or alter completely in nature. To transfigure is to change the outward appearance or form, to exalt, or to glorify (Webster's New Collegiate Dictionary). God allows us to see the glory and majesty of the Divine Son, through his transfiguration, and then leads us to lives of service. The transfiguration of Jesus is the gift of knowing him as Human and God.

Mountain climbing is not an easy task, nor is it a physically comfortable exercise. But reaching the mountaintop is an exhilarating experience. Within scripture, mountaintops have usually meant encounters with God that were also exhilarating and challenging.

The Transfiguration ends Christ's ministry in Galilee.

And now, Jesus is about to journey to the cross. His face was set toward Jerusalem (Luke 9:53). That the glory of the Lord shall be revealed is the Epiphany promise, and the transfiguration is the assurance of that power. God confirms Jesus' ministry in the presence of three disciples and two Old Testament prophets. It was on this mountain that Jesus committed himself to a course of action, confirmed by God, that would change the world forever. A few days earlier, Jesus said, "The Son of Man must undergo great suffering, and be rejected by the elders, chief priests and scribes, and be killed and on the third day be raised" (Luke 9:22).

The Gospel of Luke tells us that Jesus took Peter, James and John, and led them in the climbing of a mountain. Once on top of the mountain, Jesus was at prayer. Jesus often retreated to a secluded place for prayer. But this time while praying, he was transfigured, and Moses and Elijah appeared. The disciples, fighting off sleep, witnessed Jesus' transfiguration. The appearance of his face changed and his clothes became dazzling white. The disciples are overwhelmed by what they are witnessing. Moses and Elijah were talking with Jesus. They appeared in glory, and according to the Gospel of Luke, "were speaking of Jesus' departure, which he was about to accomplish at Jerusalem" (v. 31).

Jewish people believed that Old Testament prophets would appear at the end of normal times. They also looked constantly for false prophets who were expected to appear. So here we see Moses and Elijah, representatives of the Law and the prophets. They are present to testify that Jesus was the true Christ, to encourage him and to lift his humanity. Moses and Elijah represented the Old Testament traditions, and Christ represented the future hope, or New Testament. The traditional ways of understanding God were about to be fulfilled and expanded through grace. The solid foundation of tradition was providing the foundation for the ultimate sacrifice. This was the mountaintop experience of all mountaintop experiences.

We remember Elijah as the great prophet who had been taken up into heaven in a chariot of fire. One day as Elijah and Elisha were walking and talking about Elisha's inheritance, when suddenly they saw between them "a chariot of fire and horses of fire," and Elijah was lifted into heaven by a storm (paraphrasing 2 Kings, chapter 2, verse 11).

We remember Moses as the prophet in Israel who the Lord knew face to face. He led the children of Israel in the great Exodus from slavery in Egypt and gave us God's law, the Ten Commandments, on Mt. Sinai.

As Elijah and Moses talked with Jesus about His departure, maybe they also talked about their personal faith walk with God, as the disciples listened. Moses might have mentioned the cloud that led them through the wilderness and hung above Mt. Sinai for six days when Moses received the law, or the cloud that covered the Tabernacle when Moses met with God.

Maybe Elijah recalled the day he heard the voice of God in a cave where he had fled to save his own life, and how ravens had fed him.

Moses may have recalled the day he went up from the plains of Moab to Mount Nebo, or Mount Pisgah, and the Lord showed him the whole land. The Lord said to Moses, "This is the land of which I swore to Abraham, to Isaac and to Jacob, saying, 'I will give it to your descendants'; I have let you see it with your eyes, but you shall not cross over there." Then Moses, the servant of the Lord, died there in the land of Moab at the Lord's command and was buried in an unknown valley (Deuteronomy 34:4-6).

Maybe Elijah and Moses comforted Jesus because they knew that God's Son would leave this earth, not from a mountaintop, nor from a chariot of fire, but Jesus' way would be the way of an old rugged cross. What a revelation it would be to a Christian if he or she could go back in time just long enough to be present to overhear that conversation, to watch Elijah and Moses comfort Jesus. Can you imagine it?

Peter, James and John are listening to a momentous conversation and feeling wonderful—literally "full of wonder." They are experiencing a religious setting and atmosphere that few have ever claimed. In the heat of the moment, Peter interrupts the conversation and says to Jesus, "Master, it is good for us to be here; let us make three dwellings, one for you, one for Moses, and one for Elijah, not knowing what he said" (Luke 9:33).

Take a moment to imagine yourself in Peter's shoes that day. Peter was feeling so good he wanted to stay on top of the mountain forever. He wanted to stop everything and build houses. Don't you image that what Peter wanted most to stop was time itself? People often want to stay in comfortable places, or become complacent with past memories and hopes. It is difficult not to want to remain in situations that are inspiring, safe and welcoming.

However, Jesus knew that time was marching on, and that it was very necessary for them to go down from the mountaintop and into the valley where a cross was before him, "his face was set toward Jerusalem" (Luke 9:53). In that same valley, persecution and lonely days were also awaiting Peter, James and John.

As Peter was speaking, they were suddenly overshadowed by a cloud, which terrified them. Then, from no apparent source, they heard a voice saying, "This is my Son, my Chosen, listen to him!" After the voice ended, they found

Jesus alone. The disciples said nothing for days of what they had seen and heard that day. (Luke 9:34-36).

At the Baptism of Jesus in the Jordan River, as Jesus prayed, heaven was opened and the Holy Spirit descended upon him in bodily form like a dove. And a voice came from heaven, "You are my Son, the Beloved; with you I am well pleased" (Luke 3:21-22). And here on the mountaintop the voice says, "This is my Son, my Chosen; listen to him!" God publicly confirmed the ministry and mission of Christ.

As Christian people we must remember that Peter wanted to remain on the mountaintop forever. To remain in worship services forever, or to remain in a comfort zone forever. Let the golden moments roll on. Many people join the church, receive power from the Holy Spirit, build a dwelling right there and never move from that experience. To serve God requires that we descend from the mountaintop and serve others. Our mission is to make disciples for Jesus Christ. Christian people always remember the mission.

The commitment that we are called to make as disciples, is not to martyrdom, nor to make the journey toward death. The commitment is simply to follow Jesus, but we never truly know where the path will lead us. The Holy Spirit gives us power to be faithful unto death.

Transforming moments happen in the presence of God and a great cloud of witnesses. We have all felt transforming moments. And we have experienced a continual transition since our baptism. We have had some moments in worship, Bible study and fellowship that were mountaintop experiences. We felt God's presence, and we felt the presence of the saints who served the church in the past. Some may be stuck back on a mountaintop from years past, refusing to come down and face life's challenges. As Christian people, we accept our responsibilities of raising families, feeding the hungry, reaching out to others, visiting the imprisoned, welcoming strangers and saving lost souls.

Pulaski Heights United Methodist Church is one good example of a faith community that weekly leaves the mountaintop to serve others. Neither obstacles, criticism, nor failures have prevented Pulaski Heights from carrying out the mission of Christ locally and around the world. The Good News is that there is room for you to serve. The mission of the church transforms our lives, converts us and prepares us for eternity.

Dr. Martin Luther King Jr. talked about being on top of a mountain, but he then returned to martyrdom in the valley. He always focused on the mission of the church – to serve humanity.

On April 3, 1968, Dr. King returned to Memphis, Tennessee, with the hope of leading a peaceful march in support of sanitation workers. Just one day before his assassination, Dr. King spoke to a large crowd of people at the Memphis Masonic Temple, and he reported to the people of God that he had been to the mountaintop:

"Well, I don't know what will happen now. We've got some difficult days ahead. But it doesn't matter with me now. Because I've been to the mountaintop. And I don't mind. Like anybody, I would like to live a long life. Longevity has its place. But I'm not concerned about that now. I just want to do God's will. And He's allowed me to go up to the mountain. And I've looked over. And I've seen the promised land. I may not get there with you. But I want you to know tonight, that we, as a people will get to the promised land. And I'm happy tonight. I'm not worried about anything. I'm not fearing any man. Mine eyes have seen the glory of the coming of the Lord."

The following day, April 4, Dr. King was assassinated on the balcony of the Lorraine Hotel in Memphis. He died at St. Joseph's Hospital of a gunshot wound in the neck. (For further reading, see King Remembered by Flip Schulke.)

As Christians we listen to what Jesus has to say. "This is my Son, my Chosen; listen to him," says the voice of God. After we leave the mountain, we do not go into seclusion. We continue to listen to God through others, fasting, confession and prayer. And through the spiritual disciplines of Lent we experience God, as Human and Divine, and then come down to the valley to serve humanity.

Questions for Reflection and Meditation

• How do the transforming moments in my life guide my faith walk? Do I treasure them and remember them daily?

• Have I ever tried to imagine myself standing among my favorite Biblical characters as Peter stood among Elijah, Moses and Jesus? Take a moment to imagine the feelings that would wash over you if you could do so.

• Am I aware of transforming moments in my life? Do I remember those moments as deep blessings or do I remember them with mixed emotions? Could it be that the Holy Spirit is continuing to teach me by holding those memories in mind?

CHAPTER SEVENTEEN

The Resurrection and Eternal Life

Luke 20:27-38

Prayer: Eternal God, we thank you for the gift of life. Grant us so to hear your word that we may embrace and ever hold fast the blessed hope of everlasting life, which you have given us in our Savior Jesus Christ; who lives and reigns with you and the Holy Spirit, one God, forever and ever. Amen.

In the Gospel of Luke, chapter 20, Jesus is being tested, tried and trapped by his adversaries. First, the chief priests and the scribes came with the elders to question his authority, "Tell us, by what authority are you doing these things?" Then, they ask the question of paying taxes, "Is it lawful for us to pay taxes to the emperor, or not?"

Our text raises questions concerning the resurrection, and resurrection is not an easy subject. It is natural for us to wonder about our mortality, and/or immortality at some point in our lives. The finality of death, versus eternal life received as a gift of God, has always been an intriguing question for humanity. Some people believe in the resurrection and eternal life, and some people do not. Christian people have always spent hours each month searching for truths concerning their religion in weekly Bible study classes and personal study. You may have questions and be unclear as to what you believe or should believe. And it is quite common for Christian people to be at different points of understanding along our spiritual journeys of faith. Christians may discuss immortality in three basic terms – The Resurrection of Jesus, the Resurrection Life and the Resurrection of the Body.

The Resurrection of Jesus Christ is understood as God's raising of Jesus Christ from death to life on the third day (Sunday) after his crucifixion (Acts 4:10; 5:30; Romans 10:9). Christ is thus alive and worshiped as the risen Lord (Philippians 2:6-11) who rules the world and is present in the world and with the church (Matthew 28:20). It is a complete transformation of the physical into a spiritual body. The Resurrection Life is the new existence given to those who know the power of Jesus Christ's resurrection (Philippians 3:10) and who live in light of this reality. It is also the future life in glory, which is eternal and which comes through Jesus Christ (John 11:25). The Resurrection of the Body is the theological belief that those who will be raised from the dead by the power of God will receive a resurrection body that will exist eternally (1 Corinthians 15:35-54). The resurrection body is not a resuscitation of the former physical body but a new form of existence" (Westminster Dictionary of Theological Terms, Donald K. McKim, 1996).

Luke introduces the Sadducees as a group who came to Jesus trying to see how he would react to their questions concerning life after death, because they denied belief in resurrection. According to the Sadducees, everything God had to say to humanity was recorded in the first five books of the Old Testament: Genesis, Exodus, Leviticus, Numbers and Deuteronomy. Before their conversation with Jesus, they had found no resurrection in the first five books of the Old Testament (The Pentateuch).

Now the Pharisees, members of a different prestigious religious group, believed that there was life after death. The Sadducees and the Pharisees debated the resurrection often, each group trying to persuade the other. The Sadducees had won many debates with the Pharisees; they were accomplished debaters. We read that these proud intellects engaged Jesus in debate, asking him about a woman who has been married to more than one brother (in succession, as was very much possible under Old Testament law). They tried to trick him, asking Jesus which brother—which husband—the woman would spend eternity with in Heaven. Can't you just imagine how proud the Sadducees were for crafting such a sly trap for Jesus!   They were so carried away with their own cleverness that they did not stop with two or three brothers in their story: they supposed the woman to have been married to seven brothers in succession! They allowed that the woman might have married every one of seven brothers, remained childless throughout—and then died, only to join the whole family in Heaven.   These self-satisfied Sadducees, whose belief denied resurrection, were primed to catch Jesus by their wit.   Can't you just imagine the tension as the Sadducees let their question hang in the air?   Can't you image the distress of Jesus' followers as they awaited His reply?   No matter which brother Jesus should chose, the poor woman would have to spend eternity with a cloud of angry husbands!   As we know so well in retrospect, Jesus pointed out the error of the Sadducees by giving them the gift of a new perspective.   Jesus opened their eyes to the idea that Heaven is now limited by such earthly concerns (vv. 27-33).

Deuteronomy 25:5-10 says that if a woman's husband dies and they have no children, the husband's brother would marry the woman so the family line and property rights would be preserved.

The Sadducees take this problem to a higher level by saying this woman survived seven husbands and had no children with any of them. The Sadducees were saying that if heaven or the afterlife were going to happen, it would be like our world today, so which husband would this lady live with for the rest of eternity? In fairness to the Sadducees, they did stress living a responsible life in the present that was pleasing to God, and they denied any utopian existence after this life.

The real question for us is, what kind of relationship do we have now with God and our neighbors? Belief in resurrection life does not mean that we wait on a promise of heaven to help others or to improve our human condition. It means that we live with a different set of values and with hope everlasting. This is the promise of our Christian baptism. Jesus called his disciples to share in the baptism of his death and resurrection … "that dying and being raised with Christ, we may share in his final victory" (United Methodist Hymnal, No. 36).

We are called to build a life now that is worthy of eternity. The power of Jesus' resurrection gives us power to participate with humanity in love, reconciliation, peace, forgiveness, diversity and sharing. Resurrection faith causes us to feed the hungry, visit the sick, clothe those who have not, and to be a friend to the friendless. Hope of the resurrection life gives power to thirst for righteousness and crave justice and mercy.

The Sadducees stressed responsible living in the present because they saw nothing in the future. And to prove that there was no future, they wanted Jesus to tell them if this woman would have a husband in eternity, and, if so, which one.

Jesus responds by saying, "Those who belong to this age marry and are given in marriage; but those who are considered worthy of a place in that age and in the resurrection from the dead neither marry nor are given in marriage. Indeed they cannot die anymore, because they are like angels and are children of God, being children of the resurrection" (vv. 34-36).

Jesus is saying that life after this life will be different, but he does not give us any precise information. Most people want a clear answer, but faith is the only answer. This is what Jesus means when he says to the Sadducees, "Indeed they cannot die anymore, because they are like angels and are children of God, being children of the resurrection" (v. 36). Children of the resurrection are first people of great faith. They are people who have been given eternal vision and see life differently. Living a resurrection life in the present means serving humanity and being good stewards in the world now. Eternal life is not an extension of this life. The resurrection of the body is a complete transformation.

The apostle Paul, in 1 Corinthians 15:51-55, offers a new way to think of our mortality. He offers us "a mystery," saying that not all will die, that all will be transformed instantly, "in the twinkling of an eye," when the last trumpet sounds. Paul says that the sound of the horn will be followed by the raising of the dead in a new "imperishable" body. Paul says that believers will then be given an entirely new body that will not be subject to illness or infirmity or even death. The new body will be part of our immortal life, a gift from God, who we will join in his victory over the frail things of this world. "Death has been swallowed up in victory. Where, O death, is your victory? Where, O death, is your sting?'"

Paul does not try to explain how God will do all of this. He just believes by faith that it will happen.

After Jesus tells the Sadducees that eternal life will be different, he shows them life after death in the first five books of the Bible. Jesus quoted from the Old Testament, Exodus 3:6, using scripture that the Sadducees believed in, saying something like this, "The story of Moses and the burning bush reveals our long belief of a glorious life after this earthly life. Moses speaks of our God as the God as the God of Abraham, the God of Isaac and the God of Jacob. Paul then concludes that his God is not a God of the dead, but one who reigns over all stages of life, including the life that we mortals cannot comprehend. Ours is a God, said Paul, of all those who live in Him, regardless of mortal death. After Paul finished, some of the scribes responded, telling Paul that he had answered beyond their expectations. We are told that their grilling of the apostle was at an end (v. 37-40).

It is all right to doubt and question the resurrection of the body. Will I continue to age in the resurrection, or will I become younger? Will my eyesight, hearing loss or receding hairline improve? Will I continue having weight and serious health issues or losses to contend with? I may not have the desire to look at my physical body as it is now for eternity. What about the good relationships that I have now and the relationships that have not been so good? I may not want to remember for eternity some of the bad experiences I have had. But my hope in Christ and resurrection faith has delivered me from the fear of the unknown. I thank God for my body and the gift of life.

Paul would say that the eternal body would be better than the earthly one that it replaces. Paul asks us a question, "… do you not know that your body is a temple of the Holy Spirit within you, which you have from God, and that you are not your own? For you were bought with a price; therefore glorify God in your body" (1 Corinthians 6:19).

"But, as it is written, 'No eye has seen, nor ear heard, nor the human heart conceived, what God has prepared for those who love him'" (1 Corinthians 2:9).

It is all right to doubt and question God. In the Book of Job, chapter 14:14, he asks, "If mortals die, will they live again? All the days of my service I would wait until my release should come." The disciple Thomas said, "Unless I see the mark of the nails in his hands, and put my finger in the mark of the nails and my hand in his side, I will not believe" (John 20:25). One week later Thomas said, "My Lord and my God!" Jesus said to Thomas, "Have you believed because you have seen me? Blessed are those who have not seen and yet have come to believe."

The apostle Paul asks a great question in Romans 8: 35-39. Who, he asks, will remove the believer from the love of Christ? What pain or suffering or misfortune or calamity will separate us from the comfort of Christ's love? What principality or personal failure or enemy is strong enough to stop Christ from loving the believer? Paul concludes that there is no power strong enough to separate the believer from Christ's comforting and redeeming love. There is no dimension, perspective, event or situation powerful enough to deny God's love through Jesus Christ. "Jesus said ... 'I am the resurrection and the life. Those who believe in me, even though they die, will live, and everyone who lives and believes in me will never die'" (John 11:25).

Questions for Reflection and Meditation

• Does my daily faith journey depend only on the promise of the resurrection of my body?

• Do I, like the Sadducees, ever play mind games with God's Word? Do I try to use my cleverness to skirt the clear directives of scripture?

• Do I believe in the resurrection of the body?

CHAPTER 18

Building a Solid Foundation

Matthew 7:21-29

According to the Gospel of Matthew, the closing words to the greatest sermon ever preached by Jesus or anyone else are found in chapter seven, verses 21-29. These are the closing words of Jesus' Sermon on the Mount, which begins in chapter five and continues through chapter seven. The Sermon on the Mount is a portion of the longest recorded discourse of Jesus. It is helpful to look at the fifth chapter of the Gospel of Matthew because it gives us a brief look at some of Jesus' radical teachings before he reached our text. The fifth chapter says that when Jesus saw the crowds, he went up the mountain; and after he sat down, his disciples came to him. Then he began to teach them saying:

"Blessed are the poor in spirit, for theirs is the kingdom of heaven. Blessed are those who mourn, for they will be comforted. Blessed are the meek, for they will inherit the earth. Blessed are those who hunger and thirst for righteousness, for they will be filled. Blessed are the merciful, for they will receive mercy. Blessed are the pure in heart, for they will see God. Blessed are the peacemakers, for they will be called children of God. Blessed are those who are persecuted for righteousness' sake, for theirs is the kingdom of heaven. Blessed are you when people revile you and persecute you and utter all kinds of evil against you falsely on my account. Rejoice and be glad, for your reward is great in heaven, for in the same way they persecuted the prophets who were before you. You are the salt of the earth; but if salt has lost its taste, how can its saltiness be restored? It is no longer good for anything, but is thrown out and trampled underfoot. You are the light of the world. A city built on a hill cannot be hid. No one after lighting a lamp puts it under the bushel basket, but on the lamp stand, and it gives light to all in the house. In the same way, let your light shine before others, so that they may see your good works and give glory to your Father in heaven" (Matthew 5:1-16).

Right now, let's focus on the conclusion of this Sermon on the Mount. Some verses are troubling and difficult for the followers of Jesus, because the sermon ends with decision and judgment. The choice is one of life in Christ or life apart from Christ – building a solid foundation on Christ or making a verbal profession of faith only. Matthew wants us to know that the church is a mixed body that includes both worthy and unworthy members, and that the church is called to live a new way of righteousness that transcends Jewish law. This scripture reveals the differences between correct behavior, based only on the Law, and compassionate, righteous actions that come from the heart of a true disciple. So Jesus concludes the greatest sermon, and I paraphrase, many who call out for me, even many who call me Lord, will not make it into the Kingdom of Heaven. My Father requires that people do more than ask—even if they ask convincingly. God will answer those whose lives show that they have earnestly tried to order their lives after The Word. When the day of judgment arrives, the number of those who call out to me in vain will be very great. Many will speak in the name of the Lord, yet will not be welcomed into the Kingdom. In spite of their words, the Lord will say to many that they are strangers to him. Read the passage for yourself

(vv. 21-23).

Jesus is referring to those who call him Lord but do not obey his teachings. He explains that they should be more concerned about what they do than what they say. He rejects some of his followers because their profession of faith has been a verbal profession only. We are called to practice our Christianity as well as profess it. True Disciples of Christ believe and put their faith into action. Jesus said, "but only the one who does the will of my Father in heaven" (v. 21). Sometimes it is hard to discern God's will, but discerning the will of God begins with repentance, faith, baptism, service and constant confession of sins. "If you confess with your lips that Jesus is Lord and believe in you heart that God raised him from the dead, you will be saved. For one believes with the heart and so is justified, and one confesses with the mouth and so is saved" (Romans 10:9-10). A verbal profession alone is not enough; there must also be a commitment of the heart.

Many of Jesus' followers were concerned about keeping the Jewish law. Some were so legalistic that they lost sight of compassion, forgiveness, grace, or any concern for those who did not follow the rules exactly as they did. Legalism is salvation by keeping the law perfectly, and believing that we earn salvation by the merit of what we have said or done. Sometimes what we may think is a good work is without any authority, or outside the will of God. We might do many things in the name of Jesus, yet, according to the Gospel of Matthew, it is possible for Jesus to say: "I never knew you; go away from me, you evil doers." Doing good deeds without good intentions is faith built on sand. Helping others to help self is faith built on sand. Our obedience, if done without compassion and faith, does not earn or merit salvation. The true believer is the one who does "the will" of the Father through heartfelt personal communication with God.

Once Jesus was asked by the Pharisees when the kingdom of God was coming, and he answered, "The kingdom of God is not coming with things that can be observed; nor will they say, 'Look, here it is!' or 'There it is!' For, in fact, the kingdom of God is among you" (Luke 17:20-21). The kingdom of heaven is manifested where Jesus rules in the hearts of humanity. "Be doers of the word, and not merely hearers who deceive themselves" (James 1:22).

The words of Jesus recorded in Matthew 7:24-27 present a metaphor: Those who hear the words of assurance—the Good News that I bring—will be as secure as the wise man who chose a foundation of solid rock for his home. When rain, winds and floods tested the foundation he's made of rock, the wise man was not disappointed. His house stood firm in the storm because of the rock foundation. On the other hand, those who heard the Good News and do not respond to change their lives will be like the unwise man who builds his house on a foundation of sand and mud. When rain, winds and floods came, streams penetrated the foundation of sand and mud, causing the house to lean and fall, smashing into a thousand pieces.

The previous verses focused on saying and doing; now Jesus turns the focus to hearing and doing. Our Lord said that there was a wise person who built his house upon rock, but there was also a foolish person who built his house on sand. The person who "hears these words" and practices them, is like a wise person who built their house upon a rock. The wise person "hears these words" and "puts them into action" with obedience and righteousness.

On the other hand, those who hear the Good News and do not respond to change their lives will be like the unwise man who builds his house on a foundation of sand and mud. If "these words of mine" are not heard, if the hearing does not become the foundation of a newly-ordered life, then the future involves a "great fall." They are hearers of truth only and nothing more. The difference in the two houses was that one was built on faith in Jesus Christ, our rock, and it withstood the rain, floods and wind. The other house was built on sand, and great was its fall.

We are constantly building a personal house, a way of life. We may want to build our house where there will be no storms at all, but that would be impossible. There is no way in which any of us can prevent storms from coming into our lives, no matter how hard we may try. "Building a solid foundation" enables us to withstand personal trials and storms that come our way. We do not know when or from which direction storms will come, we only know that rain, floods and wind will come. Our faith does not protect us from the storms of sadness, sickness, sorrow, accidents, bereavements, poverty, suffering, disappointments, failures or death. In times of trial, if we have built a solid foundation, our faith in God will not fail us. Jesus said, "I have said this to you, so that in me you may have peace. In the world you face persecution. But take courage; I have conquered the world" (John 16:33).

I confess to you that there have been times in my own life when the storms of personal health and personal loss of family members have come my way, and the storms served as a wake-up call for me to reaffirm Christ as the solid foundation in my life. And now, looking back, I do not know how I would have made it without Christ. God is with us, supporting us, helping us and providing for us to live as forgiven children of God. Matthew chapter 3, verse 33 speaks directly to our priorities and our actions: look first to fulfill the requirements of the Kingdom of God, focus on His righteousness, and all of your other concerns will be taken care of. The language of this passage in the King James Version is especially beautiful and well worth memorizing.

At the conclusion of the Sermon on the Mount—consult Matthew 7:28-29—we are told that the crowds present that day found his teaching astonishing. When Jesus concluding his discourse, the crowds were silent and in awe. Jesus had spoken with great power, yet plainly and convincingly. His message had the feeling of authority, beyond what the people usually heard from teachers of the old law.

This scripture ends the Sermon on the Mount. It demonstrates to us a righteousness given rather than earned. Jesus tells his followers that it is those who "hunger and thirst for righteousness" who "will be filled." There is the way of law obedience, and there is the way of righteous compassionate actions that come from the heart of a true disciple of Jesus Christ through grace and by faith. The church is called to live a new way of righteousness that transcends Jewish law. Finding God's will is the number one priority on our journeys of faith. "Then Jesus said to the Jews who had believed in him, 'If you continue in my word, you are truly my disciples; and you will know the truth, and the truth will make you free'" (John 8:31-32).

Questions for Reflection and Meditation

- What spiritual foundations did I witness as a child? Did I see adults building their lives of foundations of stone? Of sand and mud? How did my observations at that time lead me to found my life?

- When has my life strayed from the best foundation, the words of Christ? How have I been able to get it back on track?

- How have I become aware of times when my spiritual foundation work became faulty?

CHAPTER NINETEEN

The Shepherds

Luke 2:8-20

Advent is the first Season of the church year. It includes the four Sundays before Christmas. Advent means "Coming" or "arrival," and the focus is on the birth of Jesus Christ.

This is an appropriate time to meditate upon the arrival of Jesus. We might call it, "A Christmas Story." We do well to focus on the main characters of the story: shepherds, wise men, angels, Mary, Joseph, and the Christ child. We all have heard the Christmas Story many times. The familiar Bible passages resonate in our memory. Let's look at the Shepherds, those who were the first to receive the good news of Jesus' birth. Take a few minutes to think about the life of a shepherd, the different types of shepherds, and some of the reasons why "the Angel of the Lord" gave the shepherds immediate notification.

Prayer: Gracious God, today we give thanks for the gift of the baby Jesus, help us now to hear the Christmas story, from the eyes of the shepherds. Amen.

The Gospel of Luke Chapter 2:6-7, gives us extremely humbling details about the birth of Our Lord Jesus in Bethlehem. Mary to delivers her child and places him in a manger, not too far away shepherds were living in the fields protecting their sheep at night.

When you first think of a shepherd today, some of us may think of our pastors. Pastors are sometimes called shepherds, because they lead groups of people. As an associate pastor I see myself, as more of a sheep dog than as a lead shepherd. I spend my days running around with the sheep in the field, and listening for the Shepherd's voice, and I love it. Most of us do not encounter real sheep and shepherds on a daily basis.

But when we think of a Biblical shepherd and his life in the first century, we envision a very different shepherd with a very distinctive look and lifestyle. We may envision a shepherd having a tall staff, or "shepherd's crook," a long wool cloak, hanging from his shoulders, a sling shot for protection and a flute or pipe for personal entertainment and for calming the sheep. In our imaginations we might add an animal skin bag for personal items hanging from his shoulders and maybe a sheep dog to help guide and protect the flock (Job 30:1).

Shepherding is one of the oldest occupations recorded in history, and it involves a lot of hard work. The duties of a Shepherd are to herd the sheep, provide for the needs of the sheep, and to guard the sheep. In return the shepherd will receive wool, meat, and milk to take to the market place, and/or sometimes a salary. Sheep were a large part of the economy in the first century.

Sheep are not good at finding food, or locating their flock, they must be led everywhere they go. As the shepherd leads the sheep, the shepherd is constantly watching for thieves, wolves, and natural dangers. The Shepherd might even carry a helpless lamb in his arms or in his pouch. So the shepherd works hard to keep the flock together, to keep them moving from one pasture to another and from one watering hole to another.

While the animals are grazing or drinking water, the shepherd may pass the time by playing on his pipe or flute. After eating and drinking, the animals may gather in the shade, giving the shepherd a moment to rest.

If two shepherds are at the same watering hole together, and call their sheep at the same time, all the sheep will naturally follow their own shepherd, because they know his familiar voice (John 10:3-5).

The Bible tells us that there are basically two types of Shepherds. The first type of shepherd is a sheep owner. The sheep owner tends the family flock, or the job is assigned to his children, or relatives, insuring that the sheep are well cared for. In the Bible we can read about the first shepherd Abel, and several others, Moses, David, Abraham, Rachel, and Israel.

The second type of Shepherd is one who has been hired to watch sheep. At the time of Christ's birth, hireling shepherds had a terrible reputation. Hired shepherds were often young men without any land of their own. Their job separated them from family and friends, as they roamed the hillsides keeping watch over sheep owned by someone else. It was a nomadic life.

Hired shepherds were despised because they did not attend temple services, which was the case because they were required to be with the sheep at all times. The law and local tradition dictated that no one should help heathens, or shepherds, and they were not allowed to be witnesses in the courts system. People were warned not to purchase lambs, milk, or wool, from hired shepherds because it was assumed that they may well have stolen these from their employers. The common assumption was that hired shepherds were likely thieves and robbers. A few bad hired shepherds ruined the reputation of many hard-working, decent fellows.

Our Lord Jesus, later in his life, made a distinction between the two types of shepherds. In the tenth chapter of the Gospel of John (vv 11-14), Jesus says, "I am the good shepherd, and I love my sheep, the hired shepherd does not love the sheep and runs away when they are in trouble. I know my sheep and my sheep know me."

On the night that Jesus was born, the Angel of the Lord did not give immediate notification to the high priest, other religious leaders, nor the powerful rulers of the day. Instead, the angel of the Lord gave immediate notification of Jesus' birth to shepherds who were in nearby fields watching their flock. We do not know if the shepherds were good shepherds or hired shepherds, but we do know that the average person did not trust them.

The angel stood before the shepherds whose first reaction is fear. The shepherds have to be told to set aside their fear. Only after calming the shepherds can the angel deliver the good news for all people: a Savior has been born! There has always been much speculation as to why the angel of the Lord chose to give immediate notification to shepherds.

Reason number one: The shepherds may have represented the shunned, unchurched members of society. They represented everyone who has ever been overlooked by the powerful members of society and by religious institutions. The good news of great joy was that Jesus had come into the world for everyone—especially those outside of the church. Who would be beyond the comfort of the established religious community? Perhaps working people, jobless people, people who have no money, people who have money but are overlooked. Maybe the unchurched were those with tattered clothes, those with no transportation, no friends, no status, and no property. Maybe they came from the wrong neighborhood or had the wrong color of skin.

What are we to make of God's choice to have angels deliver the good news first to shepherds, a group representative of the outcasts of society? God loves you is the good news! Because of Christ there is a seat for you at the communion table, the great banquet, the feast of life. All are welcome in Christ, and that is the good news!

Now please remember, religious people had already received notification of the birth of Jesus. The miracle birth of Jesus fulfilled Old Testament prophecy. The prophet Isaiah told the story more than 700 years before Jesus was born (Isaiah 7:14, Isaiah 9:6). The Prophet Micah told us the town where Christ would be born (Micah 5:2). The Prophet Isaiah also told the people about the passion of Christ (Isaiah 53:5).

The second reason the angel of the Lord may have given immediate notification to shepherds was because they watched over the sacrificial lambs for the temple. Could God have been telling them that they would no longer have to raise a sacrificial lamb? Jesus would be the final sacrifice and would take away the sins of all the people. We do not know this for sure; it is just pure speculation.

Lastly, perhaps the angels new that in a few years a book—the New Testament— would call Jesus, "the good shepherd," "the one shepherd, "the chief shepherd," and "the great 'shepherd." But, honestly, we do not know why the angels chose the shepherds to announce the birth of Jesus.

After the angel and a multitude of the heavenly host left the Shepherds and went back to heaven, the shepherds immediately say to one another, "Let us go now to Bethlehem and see this thing that has taken place, which the Lord has made known to us."

The shepherds did not just hear the message; they responded to the angel of the Lord's message, and then they made known what God had done in their lives: they shared their story. Jesus birth would be forever associated with all who are outside of the mainstream of society. The one who is born is our Savior, the Messiah and Lord of all creation. Mary remained quiet and treasured all these words in her heart, and the shepherds returned home praising and thanking God.

The shepherds, sometimes despised, received immediate notification of the good news of Jesus' birth. God brings Good News to the unchurched, those who find themselves outside of the inner circle. The good news for all people is that Jesus, the expected Savior, has come among us, among those who can't afford to dress in style, among those who can't afford to send their children to the best schools, among those born in the wrong neighborhood, among those who are not like everybody else. The heart and soul of the good news is that God loves us more than we will ever know. As with shepherds, God invites all people to come and see, to come and believe, to come and follow. If you decide to follow the good news like those stunned Shepherds on that night long ago, you will be able to say like the psalmist, "the Lord is my Shepherd." How better to praise and glorify God for the Christmas Story!

Questions for Reflection and Meditation

- Some shepherds were respected and some were not. How would you feel if you were a hired shepherd of good character, yet were looked down upon because of your place in society?

- How do you think those few shepherds who were first to receive the news of Jesus birth reacted after the angels disappeared? How would you have reacted?

- In what way are you—or have you ever been—considered unpopular, unlikeable, or of questionable repute?

CHAPTER TWENTY

My Soul Waits

Psalm 130

Prayer: Thank you God for opportunities to worship, fellowship and develop our faith in a land that practices religious freedom. Bless us now as we receive your word in his name. Amen.

The Book of Psalms is a refection of the many aspects of the religious experience of Israel, and it is invaluable for our use in private and public worship. Like many of you, I love the Book of Psalms because it helps me to communicate with God with power and integrity. The Book of Psalms helps me to express how I truly feel, and I experience comfort when I read from the psalms. We all have our favorite Psalms and verses.

When I am happy, I proclaim Psalm 118:24:
"This is the day that the Lord has made, let us rejoice and be glad in it."

On Sundays, I love to proclaim Psalm 122:1-2:
"I was glad when they said unto me, let us go to the house of the Lord! Our feet are standing within your gates, O Jerusalem."

In times of doubt, I proclaim Psalm 121:
"I will lift up mine eyes unto the hills, from whence cometh my help, my help comes from the Lord, who made

heaven and earth."

In times of grief, I proclaim Psalm 23:
"The Lord is my Shepherd, I shall not want ... yea though I walk ..."

Psalm 150 tells the people to praise God, to do so in His House and everywhere in his creation. It tells us that all breathing things should praise the Lord.

The Psalms have taught me how to communicate with God, and they provide for us a communication plumb line. We can learn much about humanity from Psalm 130. It is a prayer for deliverance from personal trouble, and it ends with a message of hope to all people. The psalmist is crying out to the Lord, wailing in the first six verses (which were personal), and the last two verses are a call for the people of Israel to wait and hope.

"Out of the depths I cry to you, O Lord. Lord hear my voice! Let your ears be attentive to the voice of my supplications" (vv. 1-2)!

Saint Augustine of Hippo (354-430) says of Psalm 130, "one should assess where they are and cry out to the Lord." The psalmist cries out from the depths of the chaotic waters of trouble, pain, depression, misfortune, personal guilt and separation from God. The psalmist believes God will hear him and listen. In the Old Testament, to be in a watery depth meant that one was in great distress, to the point of death. We all have moments of illness, weakness, tiredness, trouble, pain, depression, misfortune, personal guilt and separation from God. In today's world perception is reality, and after we access where we are, it is all right to cry out from the depths to the Lord! Jesus cried from the depths,

"Must this cup pass from me?" Psalm 22:1-2 says, "God, my God, why have you forsaken me?" The psalmist continues to cry out, wailing to the Lord.

"If you, O Lord, should mark iniquities, Lord, who could stand? But there is forgiveness with you, so that you may be revered (worshiped)" (Psalm 130: 3-4).

The psalmist knows and identifies himself as a sinner, guilty before God (which is the human condition). But, the psalmist also knows God's nature, which is to forgive, and he believes that God will forgive him. So he worships God with reverence, just as we worship God today.

"We confess that we have not loved you with our whole heart.

We have failed to be an obedient church.

We have not done your will,

We have broken your law,

We have rebelled against your love.

We have not loved our neighbors,

And we have not heard the cry of the needy, forgive us God."

If God were to record all our misdeeds, how could anyone stand? God does not desire for us to be burdened with our sins. We cry to God, God hears us and responds, not with judgment, but with forgiveness. In the name of Jesus Christ, you are forgiven! The psalmist knows that God is merciful by nature, so he waits for God's help. The psalmist continues to cry out, wailing to the Lord.

Verses 5 and 6 are like a chant for those who wait for God, who are conscious of their soul waiting upon his timing, who wait as patiently as watchers at a wake, knowing that the Lord's timing is not for us to understand and yet believing that "in the morning"—after the darkest hour—

our watching and waiting will be repaid in glory.

The psalmist says that his soul, his spiritual nature, waits for the Lord. And in the word of the Lord he hopes. He is waiting with an attitude of true repentance. Like a watchman over a city, the psalmist remains steadfast as those who watch for the morning. He watches with hope and expectation. Watching and waiting is hard work.

Paul Tillich, in his book, The Shaking of the Foundations (1955), says that the Old and New Testaments describe our existence in relationship to God as one of waiting. Waiting means not having, not seeing, not knowing and not grasping God; and yet having God at the same time. So, Tillich says, it is not easy to proclaim God, and at the same time, to make perfectly clear to others that we ourselves do not possess God, and that we too are waiting for God.

Some proclaim full possession of God now and are not waiting or hoping for a closer relationship with God than they have at the present time.

Tillich says that all time runs forward, both in history and in personal life, and our time is a time of waiting and expectation. Time itself is waiting, waiting not for another time, but waiting, for that which is eternal. So all time is a time of waiting for the breaking in of eternity.

The psalmist waits for the Lord like a watchman over a city; and remains steadfast as those who watch for the morning with hope and expectation. Morning was the traditional time God revealed His salvation. Christians remember that it was early on the first Easter morning that Jesus rose from the grave. The psalmist stops crying to God about himself and pleads for the people of Israel to wait and hope.

"O Israel, hope in the Lord! For with the Lord there is

steadfast love, and with him is great power to redeem. It is he who will redeem Israel from all its iniquities" (vv. 7-8).

The psalmist tells all who will listen to wait and hope in the Lord, for there is unconditional, steadfast love, and great power to redeem you, and grant you freedom from the human condition of guilt and sin. The psalmist believed that God would not only act on his behalf, but he also watched and hoped for his neighbors and prayed for their deliverance. The psalmist is waiting and hoping for the assurance of forgiveness and for the breaking in of eternity.

Verse 6 affirms the reward of the constant believer, the one who waits through the dark hours until redemption is found in the morning. We witnessed the psalmist going from the depths of personal misery and depression to waiting and hoping for forgiveness and eternity. Anyone can cry to God from the depths of life, and God will hear us and come, not with judgment, but with forgiveness. Our hope for eternity is in God, who raised Jesus Christ from the dead. "Be faithful until death, and I will give you a crown of life" (Revelation 2:10c).

Psalm 27:13-14 summarizes Psalm 130, "I had fainted, unless I had believed, to see the goodness of the Lord, in the land of the living. Wait on the Lord: be of good courage, and he shall strengthen thine heart: wait, I say, on the Lord."

Questions for Reflection and Meditation

• Do I take time to read a Psalm daily?

• Can I recite any Psalms from memory—beginning with Psalm 23?

• When have I opened the book of Psalms to find comfort in time of loss, words of appreciation in time of celebration?

• Do I have blessed hope in the future as promised by God?

CHAPTER TWENTY-ONE

The Alpha and Omega

Revelation 1:4-8

Prayer: Gracious God, we continue to give thanks to you for your steadfast love which endures forever. Bless us as we give thanks for Christ the King, and continue to reveal your presence and love to your people. Amen.

On Christ the King Sunday, the lectionary reading in Revelation 1:4b-8 reminds us that Revelation was written when the church was being persecuted by Roman authority. This book was intended as encouragement to the faithful to offer comfort in the face of adversity. The theme is that God is here for us, no matter what happens through the unreliable powers of this world. Christ the King Sunday, which is the last Sunday after Pentecost and also the last Sunday of the Christian year, is a celebration of the coming reign of Jesus Christ and the completion of creation (Book of Worship, United Methodist Church).

In order to fully understand our text, I will also refer to the first verses of chapter one. Here the writer surveys the uncertainty that Christians faced under Roman authority. He affirms that an angel was sent to provide comforting words and to remind the faithful of the word of God and the testimony of Jesus Christ. Revelation means "to reveal, an enlightening or astonishing disclosure" (Webster's Dictionary). Jesus Christ's steadfast love is the main subject of The Revelation, a book that sometimes confuses people in today's church, but was written in highly symbolic language to tell First Century Christians that they should not give up, no matter what treatment they received at the hands of Roman authorities and their rulers throughout the empire.

The Revelation was given by God to Jesus Christ and communicated through an angel to a person named John to show the people of God what must soon take place. The angel or messenger communicated by words and by visions in which John saw things that were full of symbolic meaning. He then testified to the word of God and to the testimony of Jesus Christ by reporting everything that he heard and experienced.

The Book of Revelation quickly becomes very mysterious, with angels, weird creatures, impious language and strange events happening from earth to heaven to hell. When the reading becomes difficult, scary or judgmental, the key to my understanding is to always remember the good news of The Revelation – Christ is King! God's love for all of creation wins or rules at the end of the age. Jesus was a servant to all, and the message is to go and do likewise serving one another while always living with hope and expectancy.

The early church did not have multiple copies of sacred writings, so it was a blessing to just hear the Word of God.

Verse three of chapter 1 includes a blessing of the reader as well as the hearers and all the faithful whose faith walk is energized by the text. There are seven blessings, statements of happiness or beatitudes scattered throughout the Book of Revelation, and there are seven churches. John introduces us to the sacred number seven, the symbol of wholeness and perfection. The number seven will appear more than 50 times throughout the Book of Revelation.

There are seven spirits (1:4), seven golden lamp stands (1:12), seven stars (1:16), seven flaming torches (4:5), a scroll with seven seals (5:1), the Lamb with seven horns and seven eyes (5:6), seven angels with seven trumpets (8:2), seven thunders sounded (10:3), a great red dragon with seven heads and seven diadems on his heads (12:3) and seven golden bowls (15:7). In this final book of the Bible, which represents the climax of the ages, the number seven becomes symbolic of perfection and wholeness. And when I fail to understand the symbolism, I always just remember that Christ is King!

There are seven blessings scattered throughout Revelation: blessed is the one who reads aloud the words, and blessed are those who hear (1:3), blessed are the dead that die in the Lord (14:13), blessed is the one who stays awake and is clothed (16:15), blessed are those who are invited to the marriage supper of the Lamb (19:9), blessed and holy are those who share in the first resurrection (20:6), blessed is the one who keeps the words of the prophecy (22:7), blessed are those who wash their robes, so that they will have the right to the tree of life and may enter the city by the gates (22:14).

The Book of Revelation is addressed to "the seven churches in Asia" (1:4), and these seven churches may be representative of the Church Universal. The messages to these seven churches were affirming and sometimes instructive.

To the angel of the church in Ephesus the message is that God knows and appreciates the labors, the strivings, and the patience of the saints in Ephesus. To the angel of the church in Smyrna, the text assures believers at Smyrna that the Lord hurts with the afflicted and with those in poverty, that the faithfulness of that community will be its glory in Heaven. To the angel of the church in Pergamum, the word is assurance that the loyalty of the saints there has not gone unnoticed by God. To the angel of the church in Thyatira, the message is to hold steadfast in gifts of the Spirit: love, faith, service, endurance, for God is watching over them. God makes a special point to tell the faithful at Thyatira that their growth in the Spirit—and in works—has been noted by God and recorded to their everlasting glory. A warning is delivered to the angel of the church in Sardis, telling the church members that that their backsliding—their spiritual "death"—requires an alarm so that they may have chances to return to spiritual strength and fidelity. To the angel of the church in Philadelphia, a message of access is offered, assuring the church members there that God provides an open door that no earthly power will be able to shut. God's word is that his people may feel powerless, yet they must persist in calling on the name of the Lord, even when all seems hopeless. To the angel of the church in Laodicea, the message is that of a shepherd who has not stopped calling out to his flock, that the shepherd needs his flock to circle close, rather than vacillating between straying and obedience. " Listen! I am standing at the door, knocking; if you hear my voice and open the door, I will come in to you and eat with you, and you with me ... Let anyone who has an ear listen to what the Spirit is saying to the churches."

Some may say that the primary message of the Revelation is one of judgment, but I fiercely disagree. For me, the primary message of the Book of Revelation is the love of God, as expressed through Jesus Christ, which for me overpowers the judgment. "Grace to you and peace, from him who is, and who was, and who is to come, and from the seven spirits who are before his throne" (Rev.1:4). God seeks to always comfort and strengthen His people, and God desires for us to look as far into the future as our hearts and minds will allow us, and see not judgment but grace and peace. Verse four may not be advocating universalism, but I will personally say that I serve an awesome God, who loves the entire world, and everything God created was good. God is the source of all grace, and He loves me and the world far beyond my imperfections. I am convinced that nothing will be able to ever separate me from the love of God. Verse five names Jesus Christ, and identifies Him as the one who stands next to God telling him of the faithfulness of the Church, Christ the first to die for the sins of all, and Christ the King to whom all earthly kings must eventually answer. The Bible teaches us that Jesus maintained his faithful witness even until his death on the cross. And John reminds us that Jesus is "the first-born of the dead," referring to Christ's resurrection and to the great hope of the Church, that Jesus' followers would someday experience the same.

Revelation also reveals that Christ is now seated at God's right hand, having spoiled the demonic plan by his death and resurrection. But one day, and no one knows when, Christ the King will rise through the events of the tribulation (Rev. 11:15-17), as the "ruler of the kings of the earth."

Verse six says that Jesus Christ is also the source of our royal priesthood. Every baptized Christian has a responsibility to serve God, and to serve others, because we are not complete when we serve only ourselves. This is called the "priesthood of all believers." John reveals to the seven churches that we have been freed for the purpose of serving God, and others, and "to him be glory and dominion forever and ever."

Verse seven tells us that Christ will appear in the clouds, and that his coming will be visible to all, undeniable and obvious to believers and doubters alike. The words here, "With the clouds," remind us of the report found in the Acts of the Apostles 1:9, where it is recorded that—as people observed—Christ was drawn up and taken away in a cloud, out of sight of those present. The Revelation reports that Jesus is coming to share the grace and peace of God. "And all the tribes of the earth will wail over him." The day and time of "the second coming" no one knows. So it is to be.

Lastly, verse eight says, I am the first letter of the alphabet and the last letter, ("I am the first and the last, the beginning and the end") says the Lord God, who is identified as the one who was here in the beginning, is the primary fact of present life, and the one who will be present when all others have died. Alpha and Omega are the first and last letters of the Greek alphabet. The image of Alpha and Omega— the beginning and the end of the alphabet—express the encompassing extent of God's infinite knowledge, wisdom and supremacy over the entire creation. At our church the symbols of Alpha and Omega are located on the front of the Christ candle, on the banner over the Christ candle, on the banner in front of the Altar, and to the right and left of Jesus in the center of the Rose Window over the Chancel. You may also find the symbol in other locations within our sanctuary. The Alpha and the Omega, the first and the last, represents Jesus as the Almighty One of Eternity past and future. Christ is the coming of God. When Christ returns, he is our Emmanuel (God with us). "Surely I am coming soon. Come Lord Jesus" (Rev. 22:20)!

Questions for Reflection and Meditation

- It is difficult for believers living in a society that guarantees freedom of religious expression to comprehend what it must have been like for early Christians to live with persecution. How can I appreciate what those early saints lived through?

- Is the Book of Revelation a comfort to me? If not, why not?

- Can I envision a place in today's world where Christians might need to use exotic symbols or secret language to communicate between congregations? Have I ever tried to assist persecuted Christians of my own era?

CHAPTER TWENTY-TWO

One Body With Many Members

1 Corinthians 12:12-19

Prayer: Almighty God, you have called us to serve others and given each of us unique gifts. Help us to listen, recognize our gifts and reach out to meet the needs of your world through Christ our Lord. Amen.

Ecumenical Sunday in The United Methodist Church promotes worldwide Christian unity. Ecumenicalism seeks the unity of Christians, divided for historical and doctrinal reasons, but having Jesus Christ as their point of reference. God equips each congregation and its membership to serve their community in various and unique ways. Cooperation, friendship, justice and public-mindedness create the spirit of unity by which diverse church communities can thrive and prosper as "one body with many members."

Ecumenical Sunday has two themes for churches: to pray and strive together for Christian unity, and to join together in responding to human suffering. It is important for Christians to be reminded that one church, or one individual, is no greater a part of the Body of Christ than another, because we are one in spirit. It is Jesus Christ who desires that we all see ourselves as working on the same team.

In the Gospel according to John, chapter 17:20-21, Jesus prays for his disciples. "I ask not only on behalf of these, but also on behalf of those who will believe in me through their word, that they may all be one. As you, father, are in me and I am in you, may they also be in us, so that the world may believe that you have sent me." Jesus was praying for Christian unity.

Church divisions and divisions among church members have existed since the church was founded. The church at Corinth was divided over several issues. I would like to highlight two. Some members of the Corinthian church became divided over allegiance to certain apostles, and some were concerned about their spiritual gifts – believing that some gifts were more valued or more spiritual than others. Their struggles were tearing the community apart. So the Apostle Paul writes the Corinthian church a couple of letters, detailing how they should be conducting themselves concerning these issues within the Body of Christ.

In 1 Corinthians 1:11-13, Paul confirms his knowledge of quarrels among the saints in Corinth. He says that he is aware that some believers in the Corinthian church claim to be followers of Paul, some of Apollos, some Cephas, and some Christ. Paul, clearly distraught by this development, asks pointedly if the body of Christ has been divided. This question must have hurt those to whom it was addressed. Can we imagine today being accused of splitting our loyalty between the writers of the Gospels, for instance? Later in 1 Corinthians 12:1 Paul addresses his readers as siblings—brothers and sisters—and asserts that he wants to make it perfectly clear that some members have one gift, some another, and still others have been given other gifts of the Spirit. Some Corinthians were distracted by strong persons in leadership positions, but Paul tells them that all gifts are important. Paul says there is no hierarchy of gifts among the faithful. He assures the Corinthians that, as a body needs fingers and thumbs, toes and knees, the body of Christ needs members of varying spiritual gifts. Just as First Century Christians failed to realize that they were "one body with many members," the church today can be tripped up comparing one preacher against another, one teacher versus another, one choir over another. Such comparisons were pointless in the First Century; they remain pointless today.

Paul says in 1 Corinthians chapter 12 that the ministries of individual congregations, as well as the ministries of the laity and clergy, are complementary. No ministry is more important than another:

In verses 12 through 14 and 27, Paul explains that the church is like the human body. It has many parts but it is one body. So it is with the church, says Paul. The church has many members, but all are baptized in Christ, whether they come from Jewish background or Greek, whether slave or free, we are all imbued with one Spirit. Paul celebrates the many facets of the body of Christ and insists that nobody should disrespect the diversity of the membership. The human body has many members with many different functions. So it is with the church, the Body of Christ. People become members of this body through baptism, and there are many positions within the church. Many members possess various gifts to serve the church, but all positions, all members and all gifts belong to the "one body with many members."

God calls everyone to service and various forms of leadership because there is strength in diversity. The Spirit of Christ brings different people together – Jews and Greeks, slaves or free. In other words, Jews, Gentiles, those who have nothing, those who have much – we are all made to drink of one spirit. The Spirit of Christ brings about a diversity of gifts and calls all people to belong and be unified in the "one body with many members."

The UMC Book of Discipline, Sec. 104, 1996, states that the form of ministry for each Christian is "… diverse in locale, in interest and denominational accent, yet always catholic (universal) in spirit and outreach." The Good News is that every person is capable of experiencing a sense of calling into various ministries. Feeling the call to be involved in a ministry is a sense of realizing that "this is what I must do, this is who I am and this is where I need to serve." Individuals who reach out and serve feel a deep sense of fulfillment and joy. And we are given spiritual gifts to help us on the journey.

There are four locations in the Bible that refer to more than 20 spiritual gifts. The Bible also mentions 10 or more characteristics or gifts of those who serve others. The following is a brief summary of the spiritual gifts. See if you can find one or more that you may possess: apostleship, proclamation, evangelism, miracles, shepherding, leadership, servanthood, healing, faith, teaching the faith, helping, encouragement, discernment, generosity, nurturing, mercy, wisdom, knowing, visionary leadership, managing leadership, tongues and interpretation of tongues. There are also gifts of intercession, missionary, writing, celibacy, voluntary poverty, artistry, craftsmanship, vocal music, instrumental music and hospitality. These gifts are given to us to build up the body of Christ, to reach out to others (Romans 12:6-8, 1 Corinthians 12:8-10, 1 Corinthians 12:28-30, Ephesians 4:11).

Finally, like the body, the weaker and less honorable members of the body are mixed together by God so we can care for each other. First Corinthians 12:22-26 says, "On the contrary, the members of the body that seem to be weaker are indispensable, and those members of the body that we think are less honorable we clothe with greater honor, and our less respectable members are treated with greater respect; whereas our more respectable members do not need this. But

God has so arranged the body, giving the greater honor to the inferior member, that there may be no dissension within the body, but the members may have the same care for one another. If one member suffers, all suffer together with it; if one member is honored, all rejoice together with it."

When we observe the birthday of Dr. King on January 15, we remember his vision for all people to serve and love one another. Dr. King, in his sermon titled "The Drum Major Instinct," said: "... everybody can be great, because everybody can serve. You don't have to have a college degree to serve. You don't have to make your subject and your verb agree to serve. You don't have to know about Plato and Aristotle to serve ... You only need a heart full of grace, a soul generated by love. And you can be that servant."

God is calling people to join together in responding to human suffering, and as servants to one another. There are ministry opportunities all around us in the areas of worship, Christian formation and education, mission, welcoming ministries, caring and wellness ministries, children's ministry, communication and broadcast ministries, youth ministry, music and arts ministry and administration.

As members of a church, we should support it with our prayers, presence, gifts and service. We are God's ambassadors, laity and clergy, with full authority to love and care for others.

"And now faith, hope, and love abide, these three; and the greatest of these is love" (1 Corinthians 13:13).

Questions for Reflection and Meditation

• How can I affirm the service of others that is different from mine?

• Am I aware of opportunities to work with others for the greater good?

• How can I show my appreciation for the spiritual gifts of those around me? Have I made time to make calls, write notes or send e-mails affirming my appreciation for others in my congregation who supply gifts that complement my own? Have I communicated with gift-bearers in other congregations, honoring their gifts?

CHAPTER TWENTY-THREE

The Epiphany of Our Lord Jesus

Matthew 2:1-12

Prayer: God of Grace, renew us, affirm us, and grant that all may boldly confess Jesus as Lord and Savior; who with you and the Holy Spirit lives and reigns, one God Everlasting. Amen.

The word "epiphany" means a manifestation or appearance, to reveal, to shine upon or to suddenly understand the essential nature or meaning of something. The church season of Epiphany starts each January 6 and continues until the day before Ash Wednesday, emphasizing ways Christ has been revealed to us. The Epiphany of our Lord Jesus to the entire world, as represented by the coming of the Wise Men, will be our focus.

The main point to remember about the Epiphany (or revealing) of our Lord Jesus is that God took the initiative to introduce all people to his Son, the Savior of the world, and that God continues to reach out to everyone, even until this very day. The Wise Men never would have discovered the Christ child on their own if God had not revealed his Son, the Messiah, through the Star of Bethlehem and the scriptures.

Sometimes the season of Epiphany is overlooked because it is sandwiched between two great celebrations within the Christian year – Advent, the celebration of Christmas, and Lent, the celebration of Easter. The five weeks between these two great seasons is a wonderful time to reflect on our personal relationship with God.

Please allow me to give the short version of my personal testimony of faith. I was raised in a household with one older brother (four years older), one younger sister (four years younger), my father, who is a faithful ordained minister, and my mother who was a faithful missionary. I can remember attending church from an early age, worshiping God, presenting our gifts and being with the body of believers, which always refreshed us.

I was introduced to the scriptures at a very early age. I remember hearing the story of the Wise Men for the first time when I was four or five. I can remember my Sunday school and preschool teachers telling the class this story and showing us pictures. Every child listened as the story came alive, and I believed everything in the story. I received this story as a little child. I have had my moments, days and weeks of doubt, as we all have, but I have always been blessed.

Matthew 2:1-12 is one of the foundational texts for the Christian church. The only foundational text that I feel is more important would be the Christmas story of the virgin birth of Jesus. In our text, it was "In the time of King Herod, after Jesus was born in Bethlehem of Judea, that wise men from the east came to Jerusalem."

The Wise Men from the east are thought to be astrologers, because they were guided by the stars and they are believed to be Gentiles, since they were from the east and did not know the prophecies found in the scriptures concerning the location of the Messiah's birth. Popular tradition says that there were three wise men, because of the three gifts. Some traditions say that they were kings, probably because of the scripture found in the Book of Isaiah chapter 60:3, which says, "Nations shall come to your light, and kings to the brightness of your dawn."

Post-biblical traditions have also given the Wise Men names: Caspar, Melchior and Balthazar. According to post-biblical tradition, one had black skin, one had white skin and one had skin that appeared to be reddish-brown. Three colors, three cultures, three examples representing the many nations for whom Christ came. But really, the Wise Men could have been any color and from any culture.

Once the Wise Men arrived in Jerusalem, they expected that everyone would be celebrating the newborn king. They must have been quite surprised to learn that others were not following the star. So they ask King Herod the Great:

"Where is the child who has been born king of the Jews? For we observed his star at its rising, and have come to pay him homage" (v. 2). The Star of Bethlehem, according to Matthew, led the Wise Men from the east to Jerusalem, and then to Bethlehem. Recent television special reports have explored several theological issues including the Star of Bethlehem. Several opinions and theories were shared concerning the identity of the star. Some said the Star of Bethlehem was really a comet or meteor; others say it was a couple of planets working together.

The Book of Numbers, chapter 24:17 predicts a star rising over the house of Jacob and a scepter—a rod or staff emblematic of power and authority—rising out of Israel The tradition of heavenly signs appearing about the time of Jesus' birth was seen by Matthew as a fulfillment of Old Testament prophecies.

The Wise Men give a startling report to Herod. They announced the birth of a new king of the Jews, they reported seeing a new star at its rising and they requested to pay this new king homage. King Herod's response to the news was abject fear, a fear that was shared by the whole population of Jerusalem. Jerusalem was the local base of power, Herod's power. None of Herod's court welcomed change because each one was jealous to maintain his or her position and privilege. So Herod called together all the chief priests and scribes of the people, and asked them where the Messiah was to be born.

The chief priests included the Sanhedrin, which numbered about 72 men. The scribes were the main preachers among the people who were charged with explaining the scriptures. Herod demanded from this most knowledgeable group where the Messiah was to be born according to prophecy.

They told him that scripture predicted—scripture written by the prophets hundreds of years before the fact—that the very small village of "Bethlehem of Judea" would give to the world a Son who would rise to prominence even greater than that of the temporal rulers of His day. Review the texts in Micah, chapter 5, verse 2, and Matthew, chapter 2, and verse 6.

Herod did what any ruler would do: he found some trusted agents who would search out the source of this threat to his power. He gave them a secret commission to follow the star and learn the identity of the child who presented a challenge to his throne. Herod told his secret agents to waste no effort finding the child, and then to report back to him without delay (vv.7-8).

After the Wise Men leave Herod for the second time, the Star reappears in front of them, and they follow it until it stands over the home of the Christ child, and they were overwhelmed with joy. Mary, Joseph and the Christ child were now living in a house. The family is no longer in the stable; this was not the Nativity scene.

The Wise Men entered the house, and they found the

child with his mother Mary. They knelt down and worshiped the child. Then, they opened their treasure chests and presented gifts of gold, frankincense and myrrh.

It was customary to offer presents to any great person upon visiting. They offered him presents of gold in token of his royalty (and this would also be helpful to the family, as they flee into Egypt), frankincense (an incense used in sacrificial offerings) in token of his divinity, and myrrh, perfuming ointments that represented his eventual passion or suffering for the world.

And having been warned in a dream not to return to Herod, they left for their own country by another road. Matthew 2:16 tells us that Herod was frustrated when he learned he had been tricked by his secret agents (a.k.a. the Wise Men). He ordered the killing of all children in the Bethlehem area who were under two years of age.

The main point for me to remember about the Epiphany (or revealing) of our Lord Jesus is that God took the initiative to introduce all people to the Savior of the World by the Star of Bethlehem and the scriptures. And God continues to reach out to everyone in the world, even until this very day.

God also continues to lead us, just as the Star of Bethlehem led the Wise Men. I am thankful to God for the many "stars" that have been my guiding light. Sometimes we are lead by circumstances, people or events outside of our immediate control. And sometimes we cannot fully explain what is happening within us or around us.

But we have the Word of God in sacred scripture, and we have churches with spirit-filled preaching, witnessing, caring and missions. We have the faith of other believers, and we have our personal faith and relationship with God. I will always give thanks to God for giving me "stars" to follow. Even in moments of doubt, hardship and despair, I continue to accept the Savior with childlike faith.

Isn't it comforting to read these words of the Gospel of Mark, chapter 10:13-15, where it is written that people brought little children to Jesus just so that he could touch them? When the disciples rebuked parents for overwhelming Jesus' party with young children, Jesus was not happy and—so memorably—instructed the disciples to let the little children have full access to him. "Do not stop them; for it is to such as these that the kingdom of God belongs.'"

It was then that Jesus made one of his most-quoted statements, telling his disciples that everyone who hopes to earn a share in the Kingdom of God will need to approach the Lord "as a little child;" anyone unable to approach the Lord with a child-like spirit will find entrance into the Kingdom of God impossible. Then Jesus took children into his arms and said blessings to them in the presence of their parents and His disciples.

Yes, I believe, in the virgin birth of Jesus, and I believe in the Star of Bethlehem. And "I believe that I shall [continue to] see the goodness of the Lord in the land of the living. Wait for the Lord; be strong, and let your heart take courage; wait for the Lord!" (Psalm 27:13-14).

Questions for Reflection and Meditation

• What does it mean to me to approach the Lord "as a little child?" What qualities of children would qualify a follower for entry into God's Kingdom? What qualities of children might disqualify one from entry into God's Kingdom?

• What resources do I depend on to lead me on my faith journey?

• Do I really believe in the virgin birth?

CHAPTER TWENTY-FOUR

God Will Provide!

Matthew 6:25-34

This chapter could easily have been entitled, "Do not worry, Jeff Hampton" or "What I have learned about being anxious." Worrying should not be confused with being concerned, or with good future planning. But true worrying has the potential to take on a life of its own, because there are endless opportunities for one to worry. People who sometimes worry excessively and needlessly may be defined as worrywarts. They often feel uneasy, distressed, troubled and anxious.

If worrying has consumed you to the point where you are deeply troubled and depressed, please do not hesitate to call a medical doctor or health-care professional.

Sometimes I like to worry, but recently I have grown a lot. Sometimes it is hard not to worry, if you find yourself very ill or in a difficult situation. If you find yourself worrying too much, share your anxiety with good friends, family members and your church family. I am thankful for a community of faith that responded to me with prayers and caring support, conversations, cards, emails, hugs and with the reassurance that God will provide for me. All of you have really helped me to stop worrying so much, and you have given me good advice tailored just for my personality:

Slow down, read a good book, say no when needed, pray daily, simplify and unclutter your life, take one day at a time, separate your worries from concerns, eat right, laugh more, smile Jeff Hampton, and do what your doctors tell you to do. I am grateful for people who love me and speak the truth in love to me. If your worries remain too much for you to bear, always seek help from professional medical personnel.

Within the gospels, there are approximately 60 teachings of Jesus, and the Gospel of Matthew gathers 25 of these teachings within the Sermon on the Mount. The Sermon on the Mount begins in chapter five and continues through chapter seven. Our text, Matthew 6:24-34, is a small portion of it.

Jesus goes up on the mountain to withdraw from the crowds, and his

teachings, which were addressed to his disciples over 2,000 years ago, are yet fresh and relevant today in our modern culture.

Jesus, while teaching his disciples, said in verse 25, "Therefore I tell you, do not worry about your life, what you will eat or what you will drink, or about your body, what you will wear. Is not life more than food and the body more than clothing?"

Jesus is teaching the disciples not to worry about life. God has given them life, and God will provide the means of sustaining their life. The disciples are to trust in God's ability to provide for them and for all of creation. He warns them not to worry about matters that are beyond their control. Jesus did not say please try not to worry, or you may worry if you like. Jesus said to the disciples, "Do not worry about your life," because God will provide.

Jesus then says to his disciples to consider the birds of the air; which neither sow nor reap nor gather into barns, but are still provided for by a gracious God who feeds them and clothes them gloriously. Then Jesus asks for some introspection, asking if his followers are not dearer to God than birds of the field. This passage is capped by a rhetorical question: which of us can by the energy of our worry add even an hour to our life span? (Matt. 6:26-27). Of course, the reality is that we detract hours from our lives by the tension of worry.

Jesus knew that God loves all of creation, that he will provide for the birds of the air and he will provide for the disciples. So do not worry, because you are of more value than many birds that spend their hours depending on the goodness of creation.

Jesus then told the disciples that if they decided to worry, they could not add a single hour to their life. Jesus argues that worry is a waste of time and may be harmful. Medical reports today say that prolonged worrying has the ability to give us headaches, high blood pressure and other serious health problems.

Jesus drove his point home asking -his disciples questions for which they had no answer:

• Why worry about clothing?
• Doesn't God clothe lowly birds more handsomely than we do ourselves?
• Why can't we rely on God to fulfill our basic needs?

Jesus asked the disciples why they were so concerned about their outward appearance. He explains to them that not only will God provide for their life – eating, drinking and clothing – but God will provide for the birds of the air, the lilies of the field and also for the grass of the field.

Jesus instructed them to look at the beautiful lilies of the field, and to notice how they grow without any attention from them. And then Jesus compares the magnificent robes and garments of Solomon as no match for the natural beauty of the lilies. And, if God clothes the grass of the field, which is alive today and then is used as kindling to start a fire tomorrow, God will provide clothing for you. Then Jesus asks the disciples again, "Why do you have so little faith in God's ability to provide for you?"

Jesus wanted the disciples to trust in God, believe in God and believe in God's promises. The Bible tells of a God who has consistently provided for and responded to the needs of humankind. Jesus says, "... you of little faith. Therefore do not worry ... For it is the Gentiles who strive for all these things; and indeed your heavenly Father knows that you need all these things" (vv. 30-32).

This is an important teaching! According to Matthew, the disciples were being taught by Jesus that believers have more of a foundation than unbelievers. Gentiles or non-Jewish persons were considered to be pagans or heathens who did not know the scriptures, or did not believe in the scriptures or God. So the Gentiles spent their days worrying and trying to provide for themselves. The disciples are being taught that they should know better than to worry like the Gentiles. They must trust in God to provide for them, and for the birds of the air, the lilies of the field and for the grass of the field. God will provide for his creation.

So Jesus says to the disciples this is what I would like for you to do:

"... strive first for the kingdom of God and his righteousness, and all these things will be given to you as well" (v. 33).

Jesus did not say seek only the Kingdom of God, but rather, "seek first the Kingdom of God and his righteousness; and all these things [your life, food, drink, clothing and shelter] will be added to you."

Jesus wants the disciples to make an effort to always focus first on the kingdom of God, or God's sovereign reign and rule over creation. Not only are the disciples being instructed to always recognize and obey the power and authority of God's will for their lives, but they are also to focus on God's righteousness. The disciples are being called to always maintain right relationships with others and with the creation, and to always do that which is right and just. They are being instructed to rearrange their priorities.

Jesus concludes this teaching by saying, "So do not worry about tomorrow, for tomorrow will bring worries of its own. Today's trouble is enough for today" (v. 34).

There are enough things to worry about today than to spend time and energy worrying about tomorrow. There will be trials and trouble tomorrow, but these things are beyond our control. God will provide grace and comfort for us today, as well as for tomorrow, to endure whatever comes our way.

Jesus wanted the disciples to understand that if they were to spread the gospel throughout the world, they would not have time to worry about themselves; he wanted them to focus on introducing every nation to the kingdom of God. The disciples listened to Jesus, and they learned this lesson well. I like the report found in the Gospel of Mark 6:7-9, which says that Jesus called the twelve and began to send them out two by two. He ordered them to take nothing for their journey except a staff – no bread, no money in their belts – but to wear sandals and not to put on two tunics. The disciples trusted in God's ability to provide for them.

So what does Jesus have to say about the people who really need food, clothing and shelter? What does Jesus have to say about those who are starving and homeless, locally and around the world? In this text, Jesus knew that his disciples were much too worried about materialism, which caused them to lose their focus of loving God, loving their neighbors, sharing the gospel and caring for all creation. But Jesus was also concerned about people who did not have the necessities of life for one reason or another.

In the Gospel of Mark, chapter 6:37-44, Jesus instructed the disciples to feed five thousand people who were tired and hungry from a long day of Bible study that had been taught by the disciples. The disciples wanted to send the problem away, but Jesus said to the disciples, "You give them something to eat." They told Jesus they only had five loaves and two fish. Jesus took the five loaves and the two fish, he looked up to heaven, and blessed and broke the loaves. He gave them to his disciples to set before the people, and he divided the two fish among them all.

For the people who are without food, drink, clothing and shelter, locally and around the world, Jesus continues to say, "You give them something to eat." The disciples of Jesus are to not worry and should focus first on the kingdom of God and God's righteousness. They are to do the right thing and be just, and people who are without will have all these things added unto them. Jesus is saying to humanity today: go to every nation, and feed them, cloth them, comfort them and share the Good News with them.

Jesus said in Romans 12:20-22, "if your enemies are hungry, feed them; if they are thirsty, give them something to drink. Do not be overcome by evil, but overcome evil with good."

The Gospel of John 21:15-19 contains a conversation over breakfast between Jesus and Simon Peter. Jesus asks Simon, son of John, if he loves Him "more than these?" Simon responds promptly and adamantly that surely Jesus knows how much Simon loves him. Then Jesus tells Simon to '"feed my lambs." A second time Jesus asks Simon whether he loves Him, and again Simon affirms his love for Christ. This time, Jesus tells Simon to "Tend my sheep." A third time, Jesus asks Simon, "Do you love me?" Peter was disturbed that Jesus asked him repeatedly about his affection and he said to Jesus, "Lord, how can you, from whom nothing is hidden, ask if I love you?" Jesus said to him, 'Feed my sheep.'"

The Good News is that God will provide for me, God will provide for you and God will provide for all of his creation – when we first seek the Kingdom and share with others. God will provide in this life, and in the life eternal. Glory!

Questions for Reflection and Meditation

- Have I allowed responsible concern to get out-of-hand and become needless worry? How does it reflect on my spiritual state when I do so?

- Can worry co-exist with God's grace?

- What is the greatest source of my worry, and have I shared my worry with God?

CHAPTER TWENTY-FIVE

Praise the Lord

Psalm 148

The first Sunday after Christmas is a great time to reflect on the season of Advent, before we enter a new year. During the four Sundays of Advent we are invited to first anticipate the arrival of the Christ child, and then to welcome the Christ child into our hearts as if for the very first time. We respond by giving praise and thanks to God for such an amazing gift. Psalm 148 helps us understand the true meaning of Christmas, and it explains why we are so joyful, and why we praise and give God the Glory.

Prayer: Almighty God, creator and preserver of life, all praise and glory belongs to you, through Jesus Christ our Lord. Amen.

Psalm 148 is part of the conclusion to the entire Book of Psalms. This hymn begins and ends with Hallelujah, which means Praise the Lord (or, let us Praise the Lord). It is a shout of great praise and joy to God used to encourage the worshipers. Psalm 148 is calling for all created things to praise and worship the Lord and to be all that we were created to be. This psalm also reminds us of why we should praise and worship God.

People praise the Lord in churches, homes, etc., by praying, singing and giving statements as to how God has touched their lives. We also hear about opportunities to develop one's faith. But Psalm 148 may be calling upon us to do even more!

This Psalm begins by calling for praise "from the heavens" (vv. 1-6). It continues with a call for praise "from the earth" (vv. 7-12), and it concludes by uniting "earth" and "heaven" together with a final call and gives reasons for all to join in praising the Lord (vv. 13-14). Who is to praise God?

• All those in Heaven
• All those in the heights
• All of His Angels
• All of His hosts
• The sun and the moon
• All the shining stars
• The heavens
• The waters above the heavens

Verses one through six conclude with reminders that God commanded the creation of all the elements of the world (so it is fitting that all the elements should praise Him). We are reminded that God set the parameters for every part of creation and that nothing was created except by Him.

The first call to praise in Psalm 148:1-6 calls upon the heavens to praise the Lord. When the Bible talks about praising God from the heavens, or the heights, sometimes it means the place where God dwells, and sometimes it means the sky above us. Here, it refers to both. In verse two the angels and heavenly hosts are invited to praise the Lord. In verse three the sun and moon and shining stars are invited to praise the Lord. Praise him, you highest heavens, and you waters above the heavens!

Verse five says that the heavens should praise the name of the Lord because, the Lord commanded, and they were established forever and ever. Verse six says, "the Lord created and fixed their bounds, which cannot be passed."

The Lord established the heavens, and the waters above the heavens, and fixed their purpose and their place in creation. Hymn 148 calls upon this creation to praise the Lord through fulfilling their created purpose through being. Verses 7-12 petitions the earth to join the heavens in praising the Lord. The fishes and other creatures of the ocean are commanded to praise God. Fire, hail, snow, frost, and the winds of storms are commanded to praise God. Every kind of geologic formation and every kind of tree, all of the animals of the earth and all of the people—young and old, male and female—are commanded to praise God

The earthly praise group consists of every conceivable animal, every kind of natural wonder and every type of weather. Then he adds every type of person. In short, the poet goes to exaggerated lengths of be sure we understand that everything and everyone must praise God.

The earthly list of creatures asked to give praise to the Lord pulls from Genesis 1 and its account of God's creation of the heavens and earth. Genesis 1:21 says, "So God created the great sea monsters and every living creature that moves, of every kind ... And God said that it was good." In the Genesis account of creation, God creates and shares the management or stewardship of creation with humanity. Genesis 1: 27-28 says, "So God created humankind ... and have dominion over the fish of the sea and over the birds of the air and over every living thing that moves upon the earth." Humanity has been appointed the caretakers of creation.

"Verse 13 says, "Let them praise the name of the Lord, for his name alone is exalted; his glory is above earth and heaven." Psalm 148 concludes by uniting "earth" and "heaven" together with a final call and reasons for all creation to join in praising the Lord. So let us praise the Lord!

The Lord is to be praised because the Lord's word is powerful. God spoke and everything that exists was created. The praise that comes from creation is a response to the Lord's actions in our lives. We praise the God who created by his Word. Genesis 1:6 says, "and God said, 'Let there be ...,'" and thus began creation.

John 1:1-5 tells us that the Word was present at the very start of creation, that the Word worked in concert with god, and—in fact—that the Word was God. .. All things came into being through him, and without him not one thing came into being. What can it mean that "the Word" was God? It can mean only one thing: that Jesus and the Word are one being. John also asserts that we have life, light, and hope through Jesus. Then, in a kind of benediction, John tells us that Jesus (the Light) is brilliant even in the dark and that the darkness cannot overcome him (again, the Light). Then he ends in celebration, with "Hallelujah

What does Paul tell the Colossians (vv.1:15-20)? He tells those believers that Jesus is:
- The image of a God we cannot see
- The firstborn of all creation
- The one in whom everything in heaven and on earth were created
- The creator of kingdoms, kings, and the source of all their power
- The one who formed everything we can see and everything we can only imagine
- The very first being in and of this world
- The first to experience live everlasting
- The embodiment of everything pleasing to God

Psalm 150 declares that we should "praise the Lord in his sanctuary and in his mighty firmament, for his mighty deeds and his surpassing greatness. Praise him with trumpet sound, with lute and harp, with tambourine and dance, strings and pipe and with loud clashing cymbals. Let everything that breathes praise the Lord."

When we think of worship and praise, we know that worship means different things to different people. But the praise of the Lord in this psalm is more than what happens at a special time or place. The praise and worship of creation is about living and fulfilling God's plan for our lives.

Finally, Psalm 148:14 says, "He has raised up a horn for his people, praise for all his faithful, for the people of Israel who are close to him. Praise the Lord!"

Verse 14 tells us what the Lord has done for his people. God "has raised up a horn for his people." Horns on animals are there for strength. A horn is a symbol of strength, power and victory (Deut. 33:17). The horn symbolized an animal's or human's strength and majesty. The horn also symbolized the strength, prosperity and power for all faithful people. The horn of strength that God has raised up for his people is the Christ child, the Lord Jesus Christ.

Each part of creation praises the Lord by our being. It is easy to forget about the praise that is offered the Lord beyond what we experience and hear in our own congregational worship. We praise and glorify God by being all God has created or called us to be. Sometimes we may personally forget to praise God, but somewhere, God is always being praised.

Personally, as a Christian, I praise God with all of creation, and I recognize the intimate relationship between humanity and caring for the environment. I do not litter. I try to remember to turn off lights when not in use. I believe in building green buildings when possible. I recycle when possible, and I try not to waste precious resources. I am also aware of the social justice issues concerning global ecology. I admit that I have a lot to learn, but I am aware of the debates on global warming, the climate crisis, the thawing of the tundra, reducing carbon emissions and greenhouse gases.

Psalm 148 says that all creation should work together by praising God and by doing what we were created to do. We are called to join with nature in praising God for all that God has done. All humanity continues to be called into a relationship or partnership with nature, praising God and caring for the environment as stewards who have been appointed by God.

The United Methodist Hymnal, page 246, says:

Joy to the world, the Lord is come!
Let earth receive her king.
Let every heart prepare him room
and heav'n and nature sing,
and heav'n and nature sing,
and heav'n, and heav'n and nature sing.

Questions for Reflection and Meditation

• How many ways do I praise God?

• What are the things that I am thankful for?

• Have I memorized Biblical passages that contain assurance of God's grace in my life? Have I memorized passages of favorite hymns that focus on praise for God's comfort?

CHAPTER TWENTY-SIX

The Way of the Righteous

Psalm 1

Psalm 1 is a wisdom psalm, or a meditation on life and the ways of God. It introduces the entire Book of Psalms, which was written over many centuries. The structure of Psalm 1 is clear. It presents a choice of following God, or rejecting God. The entire Psalm praises the blessedness of one who avoids the paths of the wicked and walks in the way of wisdom. Psalm 1 is a summary of the blessings of God in response to one's faithfulness. It tells us that if we have a relationship with God, we know the way of righteous or true happiness.

Prayer: Gracious God, bless us and help us to continue to always find wisdom and comfort in the Word of God. Amen.

The unknown psalmist tells us that those who follow God's path are happy. Are you happy? Many would say yes – others may say not really, but I will make it. Others might say totally happy and some may say totally unhappy.

Psalm 1 tells us that we can only be happy if we avoid the advice of ungodly people, the wicked, and if we remember His commandments and meditate on God's laws all day and all night. The psalmist first tells us what the happy or blessed person does not do. Happy people do not follow advice from those who seek after evil, or participate in criminal activities, or make fun of people's expressions of faith, whatever faith that might be. Nor do happy or blessed people belittle others who are not like them. Happy people stay away from the wicked, the criminally minded and those who look down on segments of God's creation.

The psalmist then shares with us what happy or blessed people are engaged in. "But their delight is in the law of the Lord, and on his law they meditate day and night." The happy or blessed person delights in God's Word. Happy people spend time with the Word of God personally studying, meditating upon it day and night, searching through it and living it.

Please allow me to give you a short personal tour of the Book of Psalms as experienced by Jeff Hampton:

- When I am lost and directionless, I like to read Psalm 23, "The Lord is my Shepherd, I shall not want. He makes me lie down is green pastures; he leads me beside still waters ... Surely goodness and mercy shall follow me ..."

- When I become impatient, I like to read Psalm 40, "I waited patiently for the Lord; he inclined to me and heard my cry."

- When everything is going well, I like to read Psalm 100, "Make a joyful noise to the Lord, all the earth. Worship the Lord with gladness; come into his presence with singing."

- When I become bored and forget about God's goodness, I like to read Psalm 103, "Bless the Lord, O my soul, and all that is within me, bless his holy name. Bless the Lord, O my soul, and do not forget all his benefits – who forgives all your iniquities, who heals all your diseases, who redeems your life from the pit ... who satisfies you with good as long as you live."

- When I am anxious about my children, family, friends

or the congregation, and I feel helpless, I read Psalm 121, "I lift up my eyes to the hills – from where will my help come?"

• Every Sunday for almost 30 years, in the A.M.E. Church tradition, the first words I recited in worship were from Psalm 122, "I was glad when they said to me, let us go to the house of the Lord! Our feet are standing within your gates, O Jerusalem."

• When I am overtaken by sorrow or depression, I find words of wisdom in Psalm 46, where I am reminded that God is my safe refuge, my safe harbor from the tempests of daily life, work life, and family life. Psalm 46 reminds me that "God is [my] refuge and strength, a very present help in trouble" and it reminds me to have no fear, even though the very ground I walk on might heave in earthquakes or the faces of mountains might change in landslides or the sea might turn against me in a tsunami. In spite of all those possibilities, the psalmist tells me to "be still."

• When I am tempted to do wrong, I like to read Psalm 15, where I am reminded that the Lord has invited me to sit side-by-side with Him in His tent if I can walk blamelessly, do what I know in my heart to be the right thing, and speak what I know to be the truth.

• When my faith is weak, I like to read Psalm 150, "Praise the Lord! Praise God in his sanctuary; praise him in his mighty firmament! Let everything that breathes praise the Lord! Praise the Lord!"

• When I am missing worship, I read Psalm 84, reminding myself of the beauty of God's house and the peace—

the soulful stillness—that is mine when I spend time in God's house.

The unknown psalmist tells us in Psalm 1:3 that people who study the Word of God are productive, like healthy trees in a good environment. "They are like trees planted by streams of water, which yield their fruit in its season, and their leaves do not wither. In all that they do, they prosper."

The blessed or happy person who reads and studies the Word is like a healthy tree planted close to plenty of water. They draw daily nourishment from the Word of God, which keeps them strong and healthy in the faith. They are productive like trees of great value as shelter, food and protection. They live by the fruits of the spirit: obedience, love, joy, peace, patience, kindness, goodness, faithfulness, gentleness and self-control. The blessed or happy person who delights in and meditates upon the Word becomes mature in the faith, and develops to be like Christ more each day.

The psalmist says that the wicked are the opposite of those who are happy and blessed. Verses 4-5 say, "The wicked are not so, but are like chaff that the wind drives away. Therefore, the wicked will not stand in the judgment, nor sinners in the congregation of the righteous."

The wicked are not blessed, they are not happy, they are not like a deep-rooted tree planted by water. Instead, the wicked are like "chaff that the wind blows away." Chaff is the husks or the shell, within which is the kernel of grain. During the time of the psalmist, farmers would put their grain in a blanket and bounce it up and down while there was a light breeze blowing. The heavy kernels of grain would fall in the blanket but the light chaff would be blown away. The chaff was of very little or no use to the farmer. After the harvest the chaff is disposed of or discarded. The wicked, or the chaff, will not stand in the judgment or in the congregation of the righteous. The chaff is of very little value and is considered a waste.

But the Lord watches over the way of the righteous. The word "watch" means "to guard, to protect, continuous attention, to know, to care and to love." Our relationship with God does not mean we are smiling all the time and that we are without problems. Christians endure problems and hardships every day. Some have struggles, trials and heavy burdens. We can't just brush them away and put plastic smiles on our faces. But, as Christians, we know the secret of true happiness, of true blessedness – a living relationship with our Lord Jesus Christ. God never leaves us or forsakes us. God is with us every step of the way, holding us up, encouraging us and standing by us.

Psalm 1 offers us a life with Christ or a life without Christ – a life rooted in the Word of God or a life without the Word of God. The psalm concludes with an explanation for the different destinies of the righteous and the wicked, "for the Lord watches over the way of the righteous, but the way of the wicked will perish."

Questions for Reflection and Meditation

• Is my life grounded in the righteousness that comes from God?

• Have I selected Psalms that are special to me and memorized them? Printed them on a small piece of paper and taped them to my bathroom mirror or other spot where I will read them daily?

• Am I leading a life of happiness? How can I use a few favorite Psalms to enhance my attitude each day?

CHAPTER TWENTY-SEVEN

The Prayer of Faith

James 5:13-20

The Letter of James is very small in size; it is brief—only five chapters and 106 verses. It takes about 30 minutes to read it prayerfully. James has a lot to say about how to live a Christian life. Once you have read the Letter of James you will be inspired to continue praying the prayer of faith and to do more of the Lord's work within the Christian community.

Prayer: God of all creation, your grace is truly amazing; bless us always to gather as your people and to love one another. Amen.

The author of the Letter of James is believed to be James, the brother of our Lord Jesus and the son of Mary and Joseph. James, who was once a skeptic, developed a very practical Christian position, and he became the senior pastor of the church at Jerusalem. He was one of the main leaders in the Christian movement.

James 5:13-20 is the conclusion of the Letter of James. It is difficult to appreciate these eight verses without first reviewing the content of this brief and powerful letter.

The Letter of James was written to First Century Jewish Christians, who were once part of the Jerusalem church, but were now scattered among all the nations. Many were experiencing religious persecution. James was writing to encourage them to continue growing in this new Christian faith in spite of their trials. And for James the only way to grow was to live within a Christian community, loving others and doing good works. The Letter of James says there is joy in trials and wisdom in controlling the tongue. We should hear and practice the word of God through faith and good works. It says that we should learn patience, pray the prayer of faith and help each other to remain faithful to God. The Letter of James is short, but you are mentally drained by the conclusion because you have been asked to do so much. You will not be able to do all that James asks of you, but you will be encouraged to do more.

Also, there is a small controversy with the Letter of James. Some people through the years have felt that James' letter contradicts Paul's teaching on justification by faith alone. "Justification by faith says that salvation comes to an individual by God's grace through faith. To be 'declared righteous,' or 'justified' or 'saved' is based on one's faith in Jesus Christ apart from any works of merit" (Westminster Dictionary of Theological Terms, Donald K. McKim). Through faith in Christ one is completely free from all Old Testament law, all legalism and all works to receive salvation.

I believe that the Letter of James complements Paul's teaching on justification by faith because James emphasizes that good actions will naturally flow from those who are justified by faith (or saved) and filled with the Spirit. Paul basically says the same thing in his letter to the Galatians 5:22-23: "The fruit of the Spirit is love, joy, peace, patience, kindness, generosity, faithfulness, gentleness and self-control."

The prayer of faith is not just asking for things. The prayer of faith involves sharing your joys and concerns with the God you love. We do this each Sunday: we grieve over deaths, we rejoice over births and baptisms and we empathize with those hospitalized and those who have concerns locally and around the world. Verse 13 says, "Are any among you suffering? They should pray. Are any cheerful? They should sing songs of praise."

James was following the example of his brother, our Lord Jesus, who taught his disciples about the power of daily intercessory prayer. He tells the people to seek God's comfort through prayer and praise, because he knew that many of them were exposed to daily persecution and suffering. The first question raised by James relates to how the people are feeling. "If someone is suffering, they should pray. If they are happy, they should sing songs of praise to God."

James presents conditions for healing if one is sick. The leaders of the church should be called to pray over them and anoint them with oil in the name of the Lord.

In Jesus' day olive oil was often used for medical treatment for pain and healing (Luke 10:34, the parable of the Good Samaritan). It was used in Israel to anoint priests and kings. Pouring holy oil upon them set them apart for service. Oil was a well-known symbol of healing and power. People could identify with oil, as church leaders ministered to the sick among them. The anointing with oil was encouraging, comforting and strengthening for the believer. Through the anointing of oil and the laying on of hands, the church leaders could absorb and share in the suffering of the sick and bless them with the love of Christ through a compassionate touch.

Many Christians experience all types of serious illnesses, physical and emotional. And we wonder, why me? We also sometimes wonder where is God in the mist of our suffering. At the same time we want to be faithful to the God we believe in. It is very difficult to understand this text and the unconditional nature of the promises it makes.

Another related difficult text, Matthew 18:19-20 says that a gathering of two or three Christians can earn God's attention—his very presence—by simply gathering to pray or praise Him. Read those verses in your favorite translation and share them with friends, for they promise that God hears even very small assemblies of believers.

These difficult texts appear to be saying that if the right kind of prayer is offered, we will be healed or our request granted. Yet we all know this does not happen every time we pray.

Many of us have witnessed spiritual healing after the prayer of faith. Spiritual healing should not be confused with being physically cured of a condition or illness. We have seen the chronically ill and the suffering gain a peace that surpasses all of our understanding, even though they have not been cured.

Philippians 4:5b-7 reminds us that God is never far away, but is our constant companion. We are gently reminded not to worry, but to approach every day and every task in a prayerful spirit. When we need to ask a favor of God—and who goes through a single day without wanting to ask something of God?—we are told to tell God what we need. Then, we're told, we can be at peace, we can let our guard down.

God wants us to ask for healing, believing that God is able to do what we ask. However, we are to leave the outcome with our gracious God. Jesus taught his disciples to pray, "Thy kingdom come, thy will be done, on earth as it is in heaven." We cannot fully understand God's promises, but we can pray and trust in the God we love. Our prayers are part of God's healing process, but the prayers of faith are subject to God's will.

James 5:16 says, "Therefore, confess your sins to one another, and pray for one another, so that you may be healed. The prayer of the righteous is powerful and effective."

Another condition of the prayer of faith would involve confessing our sins to one another and to God. Confession serves as the preparation for prayer and healing, and confession is good for the soul. James says that if we confess our sins, our needs and our intercessions with openness to each other, we will find strength and support for the spiritual struggles of life.

The general Confession and Pardon of the United Methodist Church, which is recited before Holy Communion, says:

"Merciful God, we confess that we have not loved you with our whole heart. We have failed to be an obedient church. We have not done your will, we have broken your law, we have rebelled against your love, we have not loved our neighbors, and we have not heard the cry of the needy. Forgive us, we pray. Free us for joyful obedience, through Jesus Christ our Lord. Amen."

Afterward, the worship leader offers a pardon to the people on behalf of Christ: "Hear the Good News: Christ died for us while we were sinners; that proves God's love toward us. In the name of Jesus Christ, you are forgiven."

The people respond: "In the name of Jesus Christ, you are forgiven.

Glory to God! Amen."

James continues by saying in verse 17: "Elijah was a human being like us, and he prayed fervently that it might not rain."

Elijah provides one of the most notable illustrations of the power and effectiveness of prayer. Elijah is bigger than life, a supernatural believer, a biblical hero. This is an example of results that are often greater than we thought were possible. The prophet Elijah encourages us with hope and faith, for which to strive.

Finally, James has one more thing for us to do, he says, "If anyone among you wanders from the truth, do not write them off, but go after them and bring them back to God." The church family is encouraged to ask people to return, or to come to church for the first time, because an authentic relationship with God includes a relationship with the community of faith.

The Book of Worship of the United Methodist Church states that: "The New Testament records that Jesus himself healed ... and sent out his disciples on ministries of healing." The Letter of James calls us also to pray for and anoint the sick, that they may be healed. Spiritual healing is God's work of offering people balance, harmony, and wholeness of body, mind and spirit – and relationships through confession, forgiveness and reconciliation. All healing is of God. The church's healing ministry in no way detracts from the gifts God gives through medicine and psychotherapy. The oil points beyond itself and those doing the anointing to the action of the Holy Spirit and the presence of the healing Christ.

We give thanks for the many church members who give unselfishly of their time and gifts to reach out to others and to petition God on their behalf. We are to ask for healing and curing, knowing that God is able to do what we ask.

2 Corinthians 12:8 says, "Three times I appealed to the Lord about this, that it would leave me, but he said to me, 'My grace is sufficient for you, for power is made perfect in weakness.'"

Questions for Reflection and Meditation

• Does my faith enable me to leave the results to God?

• Am I fully aware of the gift of God's grace in my life, both past and present?

• Am I at peace with turning my problems over to God in prayer or do I feel the need to coach God (or the church) continually to be sure I get my way?

CHAPTER TWENTY-EIGHT

Lifted Up From the Earth

John 12:20-33

Prayer: Almighty God, your love for us is truly amazing. Continue to challenge our faith responses, so we can be the best people we can be, through Jesus Christ our Lord. Amen.

On Ash Wednesday, the beginning of Lent, like many of you, I petition God for a "clean heart." Ashes are imposed on my forehead and I remember that God created me out of the dust of the earth, and I remember that it is God's gracious gift that grants everlasting life; so I repent and continue to believe in the gospel.

During this time, I practice, more so than normal, to be the best person I can be. To accomplish this, I focus on personal self-denial, the passion of Christ and the love of God. I fast, pray, meditate on God's word, and I practice unconditional acts of kindness. I anxiously anticipate Palm Sunday, Holy Week and Easter morning. The challenge for me comes the morning after Easter. Will I return to my regular Christian schedule – or do I maintain the Lenten faith response of self-denial and service?

The Gospel of John reported that the world was "going after Jesus" because he raised Lazarus from the dead and called him out of the tomb, and people who witnessed this were testifying to others.

John, in chapter 12, says that non-Jews from other countries traveled to Jerusalem so they could celebrate the Passover festival. We are told that many people approached

Philip asking to see Jesus. This request to "see Jesus" led to his last public dialogue in John's Gospel where Jesus decided to talk about his impending death.

Jesus answered them, "The hour has come for the Son of Man to be glorified. Very truly, I tell you, unless a grain of wheat falls into the earth and dies, it remains just a single grain; but if it dies, it bears much fruit." Jesus indirectly refers to his own life as the falling grain, because Jesus came to suffer and die for the sins of the world so that we might have life. The hour when Jesus is to be glorified is the hour of his death, resurrection and ascension.

Jesus also uses this image of a grain of wheat falling and dying to challenge the faith response of his followers. The glorification, the honor and high praise of Jesus would also mean dying to self, for his followers.

Jesus tells believers that we cannot be master over our own lives, and that loving our life will simply cause us to lose it. He tells believers to hate the life we have in this world, by which it seems to me that Jesus is telling us to focus on our eternal life to come. Followers of Jesus, who are able to first die unto themselves, would bear "much fruit and live for eternity." It means that we choose to lose our affection for the things of this world, and instead, focus on loving God and the things not of this world. "Whoever serves me must follow me, and where I am, there will my servant be also." Life doesn't really start until we have died to ourselves. Christian leadership was to be exercised in love and service, not with power and force. And God will honor those who truly followed in the footsteps of his Son, practicing unconditional positive regard toward others.

In the mist of this conversation with people from around the known world, Jesus explains his final decision of obedience to his Father's will. He asks "And what should I say, 'Father, save me from this hour?' No, it is for this reason that I have come to this hour. "Father, glorify your name.'" Such obedience is indeed the glorification of God. And God answers his Son, clearly identifying him and affirming him.

During the time of Jesus, people viewed death on the cross as the ultimate shame. Jesus transformed the symbol of ultimate shame, the cross, into Christ's glory. Jesus said his death on the cross would cause people from all nations to come unto him. Now is the judgment of this world, and God will throw the ruler of this world out, and the ruler of this world will lose control over the power of death – because of Jesus' life, crucifixion, resurrection and ascension. "And I, when I am lifted up from the earth, will draw all people to myself. He said this to indicate the kind of death he was to die."

The Good News for us today is, "… God so loved the world that he gave his only Son, so that everyone who believes in him may not perish but may have eternal life." All who believe may be lifted up with Christ through following him to the cross, the resurrection and then to live with him for eternity in heaven. God's love did not save anyone from suffering on this earth, or even physical death. But the faithful Christian will enjoy the presence of God now and in the life to come.

When we journey toward Palm Sunday, Holy Week and Easter morning, I am always overwhelmed by the goodness of God, and I am always thankful for all that God has done in my life and for the world. At various times, I cannot help but to feel remorse because of my personal faith responses, but I know that I can do a better job of faithfully facing the daily challenges of personal self-denial and service to others after Lent is over.

Hymn No. 59, entitled "Lift Him Up," is located in the

African-American UMC Hymnal resource called, Songs of Zion, by Johnson Oatman Jr. Verses 1- 4 say to us that our God reaches out to everyone, to people of every position and station in life, to the fortunate and unfortunate. They tell us that Jesus stands by the gate of Heaven with a key that he is ready to use when we are ready to enter the kingdom.

That inspiring hymn admonishes us to "Lift Him up" by living as we know we should, by striving to attain a standard of conduct that befits a Godly person. The refrain says, "Lift Him up, Lift Him up, Still He speaks from eternity; And I, if I be lifted up from the earth, Will draw all folk unto me."

Thanks be to God, who gives us the victory through Our Lord and Savior Jesus Christ! Amen.

Questions for Reflection and Meditation

• Does the "good news" of Easter abide with me throughout the year?

• In what ways can I do a better job of expressing my joy with God?

• What does the promise of earning new life by giving up our present life mean to me? Do I need to discuss this promise with a teacher to fully accept it?

CHAPTER TWENTY-NINE

Making Room for Hope

Psalm 146

Prayer: Eternal God, we give thanks for your presence among us always. Bless us as we feast on your word. Amen.

The Advent season, four Sundays proceeding Christmas Day, is about a God who desires to have a close relationship with humanity. There is much anticipation when we prepare to celebrate the birth of our Lord and Savior, Jesus Christ, who has come among us. It is a season of great joy, family togetherness, giving and thankfulness.

But some may fail to make room for hope during the Advent, because they are trying to figure out what this special season means, and why we are so joyous and giving. Many are too busy to make room for hope – to relax and enjoy all that the Advent season has to offer. Sometimes we just need to slow down during the good times and experience hope.

We are not talking about hope as in wishful thinking – I hope for a trip around the world, I hope to lead my company as the CEO someday, I hope to be a millionaire someday. We are talking about hope that is grounded in the promises of God. Hope as in "hope in the Lord our God, eternal hope." 1 Corinthians 13:13 says, "And now faith, hope and love abides, and the greatest of these is love." Hope is the glue that holds our faith and love for one another and God together.

So some are too busy to hope during Advent. Others are running low on hope during the holidays because they are hurting. If you have lost a loved one this past year, lost your job, or a relationship, or if you have a health problem, the holidays may cause sadness and anxiety. Please talk with someone, your pastor or friend or a professional counselor, if you are hurting or lonely. God has promised to take care of you. During difficult times reflect on the promises of God, because sometimes we do not even know that we are low on hope.

I have experienced being low on hope, not sure if God was present for me, not sure about my eternal relationship with God. Jeff Hampton's hope was reduced to 2, on a scale of 1-10, but God spoke to me, and my hope scale went from 2 to 10. God speaks to us through other people and experiences. After being mad at God, I found hope in the Lord again!

A framed message in my office reminds me daily: "Good Morning! This is God. I will be handling all of your problems today. I will not need your help. So, relax and have a great day!" I need to be reminded to place my hope in the Lord our God.

Psalm 146 tells us how to make room for hope in our daily lives during Advent Season and during good times and difficult times. Psalm 146 tells us five things we can do to make room for hope in our daily lives. Not hope as in wishful thinking, but hope that is grounded in the promises of God, hope as in hope in the Lord our God – hope as in eternal salvation!

First, Psalm 148:1-2 tells us to praise God from the depths of our heart; to praise God as long as we live—in the strength of our youth and without letting up to praise God into feeble old age

In other words, praise God with your whole life. Praise God during the good times and bad times, as long as you live.

Second, verses 3-4 tell us that no power on this earth deserves our worship: not governors or heads of state, for they can give our hearts no ease. Fellow mortals may offer temporary comfort, but their comfort often ends with their careers or positions, and certainly ends with their life. These verses are saying to not put your trust in people, in earthly things. There is comfort and support in human beings, but we cannot make our eternal happiness dependent on people. In God alone is help for eternal salvation."

Third, verses 5-6 direct us to the true source of help, the one God. If we seek comfort and tranquility, we will find it only in the true God, the one who made our world and everything that is in it. God, alone, is capable of keeping faith with us throughout our lives and throughout eternity. These verses are saying that happiness comes when we seek help from the God of Jacob, and place our hope in the Lord our God. God is the creator of the universe, who keeps faith forever. God is our eternal hope or blessed hope.

Fourth, verses 7-9 ask us about the quality of our love to others:

- Which of us works for justice for oppressed individuals and groups?

- Which of us feeds the hungry

- Who among us works to free prisoners

- Then we are asked to consider all that the Lord does around us:

- God gives sight to the blind

- God comforts the meek and unfortunate

- God loves those who walk the path Jesus set forth

- God holds close those whose lives are broken by death of a loved one, loss of many kinds, and abandonment in many forms

Our hope is in the Lord. Have hope in God's promises. He promises to:

- execute justice for the oppressed,

- feed the hungry,

- set the prisoners free,

- open the eyes of the blind,

- lift up those who are bowed down,

- love the righteous,

- watch over strangers,

- uphold the orphans and widows, and

- bring the plans of the wicked to ruin.

Fifth, verse 10 says, "The Lord will reign forever, your God, O Zion, for all generations. Praise the Lord!" God is in charge. The Lord your God will reign forever, all generations praise the Lord. Hallelujah!

Psalm 146 gives us five things we can do to maintain Hope in the Lord our God. Remember, the Lord our God will be taking care of you during the good times and during difficult times, and God will not need your help. So relax, slow down, and have hope in the Lord our God, and the promises of God.

Questions for Reflection and Meditation

• Does my connection with God fill me with hope? Am I able to feel hope for God's promises in bad times as well as in good times?

• Am I confident that God does not need my help to deliver on the promises of the Good News?

• Do I have a Psalm in my heart?

CHAPTER THIRTY

A Wonderful Meal

1 Corinthians 11:23-26

There are three main religious rites that form our faith in Christ: Holy Communion, Baptism and Confirmation. Religious customs are the glue that holds any community of faith together. These rituals are a powerful means of God's grace in our lives as Christian people. In this chapter we will take a very close look at Holy Communion because it is the central celebration of the Christian faith, commemorating our redemption by Jesus.

There are three things that United Methodists should always remember about Holy Communion. Holy Communion is: (1) a remembrance of Jesus' sacrificial death and resurrection; (2) a celebration of God's covenant of forgiveness, love and hope; (3) a source of grace that helps strengthen and renew our faith.

Prayer: Almighty God, thank you for the life and ministry of Jesus Christ. Continue to be with us as we remember how much you love us. Amen.

When we prepare to celebrate Holy Communion, we are participating in an element of Christian worship that was instituted by Jesus Christ himself. Holy Communion is a wonderful meal, in fact, it is an amazing meal. Sometimes we may experience Holy Communion as being repetitious and boring. But a better understanding of the sacrament of Holy Communion enriches our lives and helps us participate more deeply in the celebration of the risen Christ. So when you prepare to celebrate Holy Communion, ask God to give you a fresh appreciation for this special observance.

The origins of Holy Communion can be found in the Passover meal. The Jewish Passover meal commemorates God's deliverance of the Jews from slavery in Egypt. The meal consisted of bitter herbs, unleavened bread and lamb. The herbs symbolize the bitterness of slavery, and the unleavened bread and the lamb recall the people's flight from Egypt. The Passover meal is one of thanksgiving for the gifts of food, friendship and freedom. Jesus gave this practice new and deeper meaning.

On the day before the crucifixion, Jesus gathered the disciples and shared the Passover meal with them. This was the last meal Jesus shared with his disciples prior to his death. After the Passover meal, Jesus instructed the disciples to continue this rite in remembrance of him.

Then, three days after Jesus' death, two disciples met a stranger on the road to Emmaus. That night the stranger broke bread, blessed it and gave it to the disciples, and the disciples then recognized that the stranger was Jesus. The disciples said to one another, "were not our hearts burning within us while he was talking to us on the road, and while he was opening the scriptures to us?" The Last Supper meal or Holy Communion became associated with Jesus' resurrection. In the following centuries, the rite became more elaborate. It became a celebration by the minister or priest before the faithful.

Holy Communion is normally celebrated during a regular church service monthly, quarterly or weekly. The rite consists of opening prayers, proclamation of God's Word, responses and offerings, the Holy meal and the final blessing.

Through the power of the Holy Spirit, the risen and living Christ is with us as our host when we receive Communion.

During Holy Communion we use tangible and intangible signs to express the deep mystery of our redemption. The bread signifies the physical body of Christ and also the body of the church. The open table, or the invitation to all, symbolizes the fact that Jesus' sacrifice was made for all people. The cup stands for the blood of Christ and for the life of the church. The sharing of a common loaf expresses the unity of the Christian church, and the physical presence of the bread and cup reminds us that our salvation is a reality.

Today, Holy Communion or the Lord's Supper emphasizes participation by the entire congregation. After ordination, United Methodist ministers are authorized to officiate during Holy Communion, and lay persons may assist in distributing the bread and cup under the direction of the officiating minister. Every United Methodist is encouraged to receive communion when given the opportunity. Guests and people visiting from other denominations are also welcome to receive communion in a United Methodist service if they wish. We have an open table, whosoever will, let them come – including all children. Members of the United Methodist Church are also welcome to receive communion when invited to do so in any Christian church.

We gather as a community at the Lord's Table, eat from the one loaf of bread and share the one cup, symbolizing many individuals becoming one Body in Christ. Through Holy Communion, believers share in his death and experience the new life that corresponds with his resurrection. It is a community gathering, a spiritual family feast. Ephesians 2:19 says, "So then you are no longer strangers and aliens, but you are citizens with the saints and also members of the household of God." This ritual celebrates the coming together of Christians of all ages from all regions and walks of life. It is the symbolic joining of church members to each other, and to the prophets and saints of old, and to the reign of God.

There is nothing more comforting than a wonderful meal with immediate family and friends. Everything stops and time stands still, as we renew ourselves for the journey. Likewise, when we participate in Holy Communion with our church family, everything stops and time stands still, as we gather as one family – renewing ourselves for the journey. When we come to the table, there are gifts for us at each meal. The first gift is that we experience a living encounter with God. We also receive forgiveness and peace, as we are pardoned and reconciled with God and with others. We are encouraged and comforted, as we are supported in our trials and eased in our sufferings. We also experience God's grace, love and fellowship through other members of the congregation. Lastly, Holy Communion is also a time for us to present our offerings of good deeds, joys, troubles and special sacrifices to God.

When we receive the bread, we know that it is symbolic of Christ's body broken for us. "Jesus took a loaf of bread … and when he had given thanks; he broke the bread, and said, 'This is my body which is for you.'" The bread speaks to us both of Christ's suffering and his ability to sustain us.

So as you dip the bread into the cup, remember, "In the same way Our Lord Jesus took the cup, also after supper, saying, 'this cup is the new covenant in my blood. Do this, as often as you drink it, in remembrance of me.'" After receiving the bread and cup, we respond, "Amen," "Thanks Be to God," "Glory to God" or any other expression of gratitude. Jesus concluded the supper by saying, "For as often as you eat this bread, and drink the cup, you proclaim the Lord's death until he comes."

Peter 1:18-19 speaks to us of hope in Christ Jesus. The writer reminds us that we have been ransomed from the futility of earthy ways—including the ways of our forebears—and invites us to rely solely upon "the precious blood of Christ." In Christ, we are considered to be blameless, our character is judged to be faultless.

Under this New Covenant of grace, our redemption does not depend upon our works. Our redemption depends upon the grace of Jesus. In this New Covenant of grace, we now live for Christ by letting Christ live in us.

In summary, the Good News is that Holy Communion has three main components – remembrance, forgiveness and grace.

"For God so loved the world that he gave his only Son, so that everyone who believes in him may not perish, but may have eternal life" (John 3:16).

This meal reminds us that we are Easter people. Christ Is Risen! Christ Is Risen Indeed!

Questions for Reflection and Meditation

• Am I participating in Holy Communion as often as I should? When participating, am I able to do so in a prayerful state, focusing on the meaning of the sacrament?

• Am I a member of a small group of supportive friends who are not family members?

• Do I sometimes stop in my busy life to remember that I have been ransomed from the futility of earthly ways?

CHAPTER THIRTY-ONE

Work Out Your Own Salvation

Philippians 2:1-13

The apostle Paul wrote to the Christian believers at Philippi from a jail cell. He was often imprisoned, flogged, beaten with rods, and stoned. He experienced three shipwrecks. Hunger and thirst were constant companions. Often, he was pursued by those who would take his life (2 Corinthians 11:23-29). After more than 20 years, he finds himself sitting in jail feeling defeated.

However, at the same time he feels the joy of serving God. Paul discovers encouragement in Christ, the redeeming love of Christ and he feels he has been showered with a rich share of the Holy Spirit. From his jail cell he invites the Christians at Philippi to find this same encouragement and Christian unity of mind and love in Christ, which would certainly make his joy complete.

Paul instructs the Philippians to "work out their salvation in fear and trembling." Salvation refers to God working in the life of the believer to bring that person into harmony with God through Christ. Our salvation includes forgiveness from our sins and their consequences. Good works refers to "actions that emerge in Christians as a result of the Holy Spirit's activity. They are a response to God's grace in Christ and are acts of love, care and justice that render practical service to others" (Westminster Dictionary of Theological Terms, Donald K. McKim).

Paul is not saying that we should work for our salvation – because we do not earn salvation. Our salvation does not depend on our personal abilities or actions. As Christian people we accept the gift of salvation by faith. God wants us to respond to the salvation that has been freely given to us through Jesus Christ. We do not work for salvation, but we are to work out our salvation. If you have worked out your salvation, it means that you have brought your salvation to a practical expression.

As Christians we are in the process of changing. Each day I personally struggle with my response to the grace of God in my life, and how that grace should manifest itself in my daily life as a Christian. I have experienced times of rapid growth and periods of idleness, but I know that I am changing. My personal faith struggles at various times may include daily Bible reading, personal prayer, daily devotion, service to those who can not serve me in return, reconciling with friends, family and others I may not understand and showing concern, love, compassion, kindness, generosity and faithfulness toward humanity in general. Paul reminds me that living the Christian life requires tremendous seriousness as I work out my salvation. The end result should be a closer relationship with God, family, church, neighbors and a better world that starts with me. The Good News is that God is at work in me, enabling me daily to work for God's good pleasure.

The Christian faith is radical to popular culture and intensely practical. Paul shares good theology, and he tells us how to practice our faith. It is not what we profess, but what we practice as a response to this free act of God's Grace, that makes us Christians. God wants our salvation to be worked out into daily expressions within our actions and relationships. We need to take intentional steps in order to ensure our spiritual development. The Good News is that God is at work in each of us to enable us to work out our salvation.

In 1963, Dr. Martin Luther King Jr. was imprisoned like the Apostle Paul for expressing Christian values, and like Paul, Dr. King was detained many times. Please allow me to share a portion of Dr. King's letter.

On April 16, 1963, Dr. King wrote a letter to "fellow clergymen" while confined in the Birmingham city jail for nonviolent direct-action protest and civil disobedience of morally wrong laws. Dr. King was responding to statements calling him an extremist, and his activities "unwise and untimely."

Dr. King wrote, "Seldom do I pause to answer criticism of my work and ideas ... I am in Birmingham because injustice is here. We began a series of workshops on nonviolence and we repeatedly asked ourselves: 'Are you able to accept blows without retaliating?' 'Are you able to endure the ordeal of jail?' But though I was initially disappointed at being categorized as an extremist, as I continued to think about the matter, I gradually gained a measure of satisfaction from the label. Was not Jesus an extremist for love? 'Love your enemies, bless them that curse you, do good to them that hate you, and pray for them which despitefully use you, and persecute you.' Was not Amos an extremist for justice? 'Let justice roll down like waters and righteousness like an ever-flowing stream.' Was not Paul an extremist for the Christian gospel? 'I bear in my body the marks of the Lord Jesus.' So the question is not whether we will be extremists, but what kind of extremists we will be. Will we be extremists for hate or for love? Will we be extremists for the preservation of injustice or for the extension of justice? In that dramatic scene on Calvary's hill three men were crucified. We must never forget that all three were crucified for the same crime – the crime of extremism. Two were extremists for immorality, and thus fell below their environment. The other, Jesus Christ, was an extremist for love, truth and goodness, and thereby rose above his environment" (Letter From Birmingham Jail, April 16, 1963).

Because of Christ, we can fellowship with the Holy Spirit, which dwells within each of us. Paul encouraged a community of humility where everyone treated others as if they were better than themselves. He envisioned a "caring community" where people considered the needs of others before considering their own needs. As Christians we do not all think the same thoughts or always have the same opinions, but we all love God "in full accord." We care for and pray for our sisters and brothers wherever they may be – neighbors next door, across town, in the next state or around the world.

Paul was saying to the Philippians, "if you have gotten anything at all out of following Christ, if his love has made any difference in your life, then agree with each other, love each other and be friends. Put self aside, reach out to one another, your community, the world and help others" (Philippians 2:1-2, paraphrased).

Paul reminds us that Jesus humbled himself and became obedient to the point of death, even death on a cross (v. 8). "These verses were part of an early Christian hymn to remind the Christians of the starting point of their own faith (Interpreter's One Volume Commentary, 1997). In his argument for Christian unity, Paul gave the powerful example of our Lord Jesus on the cross. In his argument for Christian values, Dr. King gave the powerful example of our Lord Jesus on the cross. Christians should have the same attitude that Jesus had when he went to the cross for us – a sacrificial attitude. Jesus is the greatest example of sacrificial living. He lived an obedient life, always thinking of others, and died an obedient death, thinking of others. Jesus counted the cost, and he freely gave his life for all creation, giving us the perfect model for Christian discipleship. "For God so loved the world that he gave his only Son, so that everyone who believes in him may not perish but may have eternal life" (John 3:16). Jesus is alive today, and his name is above every other name (v. 9). As Christian people we offer our prayers in Jesus' name. The Gospel of John 14:13-14 says, "I will do whatever you ask in my name, so that the Father may be glorified in the Son. If in my name you ask me for anything, I will do it."

Finally, Paul tells the Philippians what they must do to maintain Christian unity and vitality: Addressing the "beloved," Paul tells the saints at Philippi, and by inference he tells us, that we must take charge of our own salvation "with fear and trembling." Paul reminds us that we must be pro-active in our spiritual life, attentive to God working within our lives, making our feeble efforts more fruitful than we can imagine (vv. 12-13).

Paul wanted the Philippians to continue in the faith as they had in the past, when he had been with them. God is at work in us through the Holy Spirit, to give us the power to act according to God's good pleasure. Jesus told the disciples that when he went away, they were to go to Jerusalem and wait until power came from on high.

God is the one who gives us the desire to follow him. God saves us because of his mercy, not because of good works. God is also the person who gives us the ability to perform acts of goodness. God loves and forgives us completely, and we respond by forgiving, loving and helping others. Through the process of salvation we become more and more like Jesus daily.

We continuously work out our salvation by renewing

our spiritual strength through reading, music, Bible study with others, constant personal devotions, spiritual diaries and participation in small groups that are accountable to one another. We are open to new opportunities for growing in faith, and we allow God to use us daily. As believers we are partners with God, working together.

The Good News is that God would ultimately resolve the broken relationships at Philippi, and God will ultimately resolve any brokenness that we have within our church, our families, with friends and with those whom we may not understand. Ephesians 2:8-9 says, "For by grace you have been saved through faith, and this is not your own doing; it is the gift of God – not the result of works, so that no one may boast."

The Apostle Paul concluded his letter to the Christians at Philippi with powerful assurances, saying—in effect— that God will take care of us better than we could possibly take care of ourselves, that God will attend to our needs, both spoken and unspoken. How can God do this? Because God has prepared a bounty of spiritual riches for us through Christ Jesus. We belong to God, Paul reminds us, now and forever (Philippians 4:19-20).

Dr. King concluded his letter from the Birmingham city jail with these words, "I hope this letter finds you strong in the faith. I also hope that circumstances will soon make it possible for me to meet each of you, not as an integrationist or a civil rights leader, but as a fellow clergyman and a Christian brother ... and in some not too distant tomorrow, the radiant stars of love and brotherhood will shine over our great nation with all their scintillating beauty. Yours for the cause of peace and brotherhood, Martin Luther King Jr."

God develops compassion within each of us regardless of our age, race, color, sexual orientation, physical condition or economic status. And we respond to God's grace through our prayers, our presence, our gifts and our service.

Writing to the Romans in the first verses of chapter 12, Paul appealed to the brothers and sisters of the faith to become a "living sacrifice, holy and acceptable to God," and to count that process as an act of worship. Paul went on to advise maintaining a distance from the powers and influences of this mortal life, encouraging believers to "renew your minds" and meditate constantly on the will of God, focusing on preparing our souls as near to God's perfection as we can.

Questions for Reflection and Meditation

• How am I working out my own salvation?

• Do I every take time out to imagine the blessings that God is preparing for me in Heaven?

• Can I imagine being in a jail cell—because of our faith practice—as Paul was near the end of his ministry?

• Am I involved in any mission projects or service organizations?

About The Author

The Rev. Dr. Jeffery B. Hampton is associate/executive pastor in charge of Caring Ministries and the program staff at Pulaski Heights United Methodist Church, a 4,000-member congregation, in Little Rock, Arkansas. Dr. Hampton is a cum laude graduate with a Bachelor of Arts degree in Sociology from Morris Brown College in Atlanta. He earned a Master of Divinity and a Doctor of Ministry from Memphis Theological Seminary.

Dr. Hampton's pastoral career includes appointments to Greater St. Mark A.M.E. Church in Thornton, Arkansas; St. Paul A.M.E. Church in Newport, Arkansas; The Ebenezer UMC Conway- Mount Zion Center Ridge- Wesley UMC Morrilton Charge; McCabe Chapel UMC in North Little Rock, and Pulaski Heights UMC in Little Rock.

He also served as adjunct professor of philosophy and religion at the University of Arkansas at Pine Bluff Extension Campus – Shorter College in North Little Rock. Dr. Hampton is a Disciple Bible Study, and Christian Believer Bible Study leader. He has completed studies in building covenantal relationships, small group finances, Shalom Leadership, Stephen Ministry Leadership, marriage, and grief counseling.

Dr. Hampton and his wife, Cynthia Ann Puckett Hampton, have two daughters, Joya and Cheyanne.

"Be faithful until death, and I will give you the crown of life" (Revelation 2:10c) is a scripture that guides Dr. Hampton's ministry. He is committed to serving God through making disciples for Jesus Christ and advancing multicultural opportunities in the church, community and world.